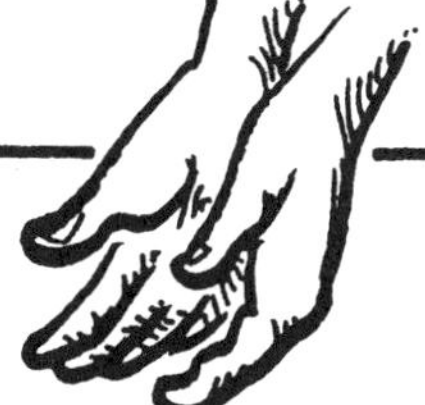

Richard Austin Thompson

Illustrations by Theresa Bayer.

ISBN Number 0-9646915-0-7

Library of Congress Catalog-in-Publication Number 95-77351

Printed in the United States of America
at Morgan Printing in Austin, Texas

Dedicated to my wife,
Margaret Ormsby Thompson

Table of Contents

Introduction

"Preaching the Practice" was a concept which presented itself to me in 1986, a year of pastoral transition. At that time I had completed twenty seven years of ministry, including early years in a small town near Tulsa, Oklahoma and twenty two years in a Chicago suburb. During my Illinois pastorate I edited and wrote for *The Journal of The Academy of Parish Clergy* over a two year period. This journalistic service was evidence of a growing interest in sharing and comparing professional experience.

It happened that my move in the mid-80s brought me to Austin, Texas where *The Clergy Journal* was being published. That proximity and the openness to my writing by the then Publisher/Editor Manfred Holck, Jr. proved to be the catalyst for my submitting articles. These pieces have been published in that periodical since 1988.

Fourteen of the chapters contained in this volume were originally published in *The Clergy Journal*, with the remaining articles to be published in altered form at a future date. The current President/Publisher Pete Velander and Executive Editor Clyde Steckel have been most cooperative in facilitating my converting this material into book form.

By transposing the saying "Practice what your preach!," I have sought to show how preaching could and should give expression to the various aspects of parish practice. I began each of the articles in the series and each of the following chapters with the practice because it is the daily exercise of ministry which provides the context for the homiletical task.

While the chapters are organized by alphabetical listing of pastoral practices, there are three organizing concepts which have emerged in the preparation of the material: functions, dimensions, and specialities.

Functions are those basic leadership tasks of clergy—Worship (including the one on Worship itself, on Funerals, on Preaching, and on Weddings), Education, Caring, Outreach, Social Ministry, and Stewardship. Dimensions are those aspects of ministry which cut across all functions, including Administration, Communications, Conflict Resolution, Fellowship, Humor, and Teamwork. Specialties represent those particular interests and skills which give unique quality to a pastor's practice. In my case these have included Local History, Media Ministry, and Storytelling.

To be sure, there may debate over whether these categories are inclusive enough or whether they are mutually exclusive. But, hopefully, this division of topics will serve as a stimulus for readers to reflect upon the diversity and richness of parish practice.

It has been my pleasure to work with illustrator Theresa Bayer. Her lively drawings throughout the text give a light and graceful touch to the whole.

A special word of special appreciation must, of course, be extended to the members in the churches which I have served for over three and a half decades. The variety of settings has provided a rich diversity in which to minister. The good folks in First Presbyterian Church of Bristow, Oklahoma, in Southminster Presbyterian Church in Glen Ellyn, Illinois, and most recently at Central Presbyterian Church in Austin, Texas, have kindly and patiently allowed me to exercise ministry with them in preaching, in practice and in the heart.

I am also indebted to those who have taken the time to read the manuscript and to offer helpful responses. Among these are Chuck Meyer, Director of Pastoral Services at St. David's Hospital in Austin, Peter Hawkins and David Kelsey, both of the Yale Divinity School faculty in New Haven Connecticut, Deborah Jarvis, Pastor of Bethel United Church of Christ in Elmhurst, Illinois.

The credits would not be complete without acknowledging the grace of God represented by and extended through my family. It is not possible to identify exactly where the influence to write, preach and practice began. Elbert Hubbard, whose turn-of-the-century publications included "Message to Garcia," is an ancestor on my father's side. Less well known on my mother's side but another contributor to the gene pool was my great uncle Dan Wooley, an 1870's pioneer to Texas and a Republican who wrote for The Marlin Democrat! My mother herself, while not a published author, has from the beginning provided the spiritual sensitivity which contributed greatly to my decision to enter the ministry.

My wife Margaret has "been there" for me in every way over nearly forty years of marriage. She has provided a clergy spouse model which has inspired each of the congregations I have served. She has participated as a committed lay person, while in no way seeking to be an unofficial "Assistant Pastor." By being her own person, by creatively parenting our two sons, by developing her own career as an attorney while providing unconditional love and support to her husband—all of that beautiful balance is what leads me to dedicate this book to her.

Administration

The Practice

"Administrivia" is the pejorative way that organizational life has come to be described. While often handled trivially in the church, administration, at its heart, is "ministry." That aspect of parish life may be no less a source of blessing than preaching, teaching, or doing mission work.

The scriptural basis for that perspective is 1 Corinthians 12:28 where Paul identifies administration as one of the gifts of the Spirit. Now, as then, when a religious community is well organized, people are enabled to realize their spiritual potential and enjoy good *esprit de corps*. When corporate life is poorly organized, then people feel that their time has been wasted and become discouraged.

Toward the development of creative administration, it will prove helpful to identify what may be termed as "The Three P's" of sound organization: purpose, policy, process. While every organization, whether secular or sacred, will function within these dimensions, the faith community provides special meaning for each, as the following analysis will suggest.

Purpose

Theologically, purpose is the starting point, as implied by the very pattern of the universe itself. Faith in the Creator who brings order out of chaos translates into meaningful human experience. To be made in God's image is to proceed according to plan.

Likewise does the well organized church begin with a clear sense of its own identity. Perhaps more revealing in this regard than a formal mission statement is a congregation's brochure which sets forth the primary activities of the congregation. Built into that interpretative piece may be the fundamental rationale for the community's existence.

As may be said of an individual so of a group, "No wind is favorable to the ship which has no port." While all faith communities exist for worship, education and ministry, each must have a special niche to fill in exercising those basic activities or it will cease to be.

Flowing from purpose are goals and objectives. According to organizational theory, the former are usually established a few at a time for a one to three year period. Having served a term on a school board, I discovered that even such a tightly-articulated structure does well to have no more than three or four goals within a three year time–frame. The objectives are what may be achieved within a year or so. Staff and organizational goals are, ideally, as coordinated as they are clearly defined.

Within a church setting this procedure is not always that neatly followed. Yet there may be movement in the direction of intentionally defining measurable results which provides a sense of momentum. One essential means toward meeting those ends is in terms of the second dimension of organizational life.

Policies

Policies are the framework within which purposes are implemented. Sometimes church policies are like the "unwritten constitution" of Great Britain, with decisions made according to traditions. But committing them to writing insures consistency and saves the grief of having to act on an "ad hoc" basis.

If a denomination has a constitution, then the broadest framework is in place. A congregation needs by-laws to describe local procedure for officer selection, dates of congregational meetings and to define its corporate relationship to the state.

A policy manual for the governing board is essential in regard to several critical areas of congregational life. Personnel policies guarantee uniformity of treatment among employees and thereby foster good staff morale. Use of the property and defining sound financial practice are other issues which will be included in such a manual. While not often identified as such, the annual budget is a primary policy statement as it implicitly expresses a church's priorities at any given point in time. Yet for all the need of clear statements of purpose and policies, no less essential is the third dimension to which we come finally.

Process

Since it's as much how things are done as what is done that makes for good working relationships, the process of group life requires careful attention. An administration committee is the coordinating group which nurtures goal setting, leads in policy formulation, and is the on-going agent for monitoring the process. The committee fittingly leads in an annual officers' retreat which often proves to be key in coordinating efforts, in planning ahead, and in being intentional about the way meetings are conducted.

A recent officers' retreat in the church I serve offers an example of how to be deliberative about the way people do business in the church. Among the issues raised was how to deal with conflict positively by recognizing the value of difference, and by learning to disagree agreeably. Among the other questions probed as to what constitutes the "magic meeting" were these:

What makes for a spiritually beneficial meeting, not only with beginning devotionals but throughout the whole of the gathering?

How do you determine the balance between too much and too little paper in mail-outs ahead of time?

Ought officers to be expected to prepare ahead of time by reading the materials?

Should the board ever do a committee's work?

Should discussion be limited to motions?

Should Roberts' Rules of Order be the only procedural guideline? When and where is "brainstorming" appropriate?

What is the fitting relationship between clergy and lay leadership.

Conclusion

Certainly a fitting conclusion to these reflections on administration as an expression of ministry is that reflections at the end of a meeting are important. A skilled facilitator might be designated as the one to review not only what happened during the course of discussion, but how that interaction transpired.

As has been said of sermons so of meetings, that all end but not all conclude. May the endings as well as the beginnings occur gracefully.

The Preaching

WELL ORGANIZED

I Corinthians 12:27-31

It was in the years of John F. Kennedy's presidency that the biblical term "charisma" came into vogue. It has popularly been identified with a leader's personal magnetism.

But in the New Testament setting, charisma meant "gifts of the Spirit." It was closer to what has more recently been called charismatic churches—where people speak in tongues. In fact that was the issue with which Paul was wrestling at the time he wrote his letters to the church at Corinth. Glossolalia, as these outpourings of the Spirit have also been termed, was threatening to tear apart the early faith community. For charismatics were claiming to be more spiritual than those who had not been so carried away in their enthusiasm.

In response to that purported superiority Paul penned this letter calling for mutual appreciation for a variety of spiritual gifts. They do indeed all seem spiritual, except one: administration.

How Spiritual?

That talent appears out of place in this sequence which includes preaching, teaching and healing. For administrators are commonly pictured as bureaucrats who draw higher salaries, but who aren't as essential to an operation as those on the front-line.

There's a story to this effect about a bird dog named "Ole Blue" whom one hunter always asked for when the season opened. But one year the owner deflected the request for "Ole Blue" saying, "Oh, you don't want him. He's not any good anymore." When the hunter seemed puzzled after having always bagged his limit in previous years with the help of that animal, the owner explained, "We made the mistake since you were here last of changing his name to `Administrator.' Now all he does is sit around and bark at the other dogs!"

Granted that this stereotypical view of administrators may have some truth it it, the fact is that the apostle lists this position among others necessary for the work of Spirit-filled ministry.

Hurray for Organized Religion!

This is an especially important message in an age when "organized religion" is getting such a bad rap. Certainly over-organization can stifle the Spirit. But disorganized religion is worse yet. Leaders may so poorly administer churches that members are left unrecruited, underutilized, and even at times exploited. When too few are carrying too much of the load, burn-out beckons. When there are plenty of volunteers, but no one is willing or able to give directions, then chaos lurks. When power becomes concentrated or unaccounted for, then the congregation is a easy prey for dishonest practices.

It helps to look beneath the surface of the word for "administrator" in scripture to get a sense of how critical is that role. The Greek term is *kuberneseis,* meaning a ship's pilot who steers the boat through the rocks and shoals to harbor. While administration is often a routine matter, the underlying task of directing, whether the Ship of State or simply the vessel of a local congregation, it is a vital one indeed.

Now according to recent management theory, there are two styles of administration: the captain of the ship and the *laissez faire* models. One is highly directive, as when a boat is sinking it is no time to take a vote. The other is enabling group members to take the lead or to fulfill their roles otherwise.

Yet even as circumstances dictate varying styles, the underlying principle is the same: that the Body of Christ belongs to God; not to clergy, not to any given generation of laity, but to God. We are but stewards, as are all administrators and managers accountable to the owner.

Marks of a Gifted Administrator

Consequently the gift of administration is exercised first and foremost in a spirit of humility, not with any delusions of grandeur nor out of some compulsive need "to lord it over" others. Yet guarding against the misuse of power is only a starting point for responsible administration. To be Spirit-filled as an administrator is to be gifted with vision and problem-solving abilities. What a rare combination! To be both creative and practical!

While we have heard "the vision thing" discounted at the highest levels of government, the fact is as suggested in I Samuel that people languished when "there was no frequent vision." Consequently it is no accident that Jesus' father, as Jesus was himself, a dreamer. The Kingdom of God, in its ever-varied forms, comes through the imagination of those able to see beyond the ends of their noses.

But how to combine that Martin Luther King, Jr., "I have a dream" visionary capacity with ability to set priorities, formulate plans, and implement them efficiently? Jesus, as a carpenter's son, also knew how to get things done. He not only went "to prepare a place" for us eternally, but did so in very earthy ways, as evidenced in his making arrangements for the upper room. So it is that the sacrament is fittingly administered in his name. Jesus was the embodiment of the good administrator.

Paul compared him to the body's head, which gives direction to the whole. Our response to his call is to exercise those capabilities fully if we have been granted them, or to support those gifts if we discern them in others. The purpose of so doing things "decently and in order," as the Presbyterians term it, is not to have tidy desks or to shuffle paper, but to have more time, talent and treasure to share with others.

Truly can we hope that we will increasingly become a faith community in which each of us knows the role that he or she is to play, with a willingness to play it, and with anticipation of how our individual efforts can contribute to a well orchestrated whole. The wholistic metaphor which Paul uses for the church has been given added dimension as we have learned more about the human body from modern biology, as described in a *Life* magazine feature:

> As he soars across the stage in a single vaulting step a dancer moves with the smoothness no machine can match and no flow chart can capture. This is the way your body moves in its more prosaic moments—when you hop up a step or jump across a puddle. It is composed of some 100 organs, 20 bones, 600 muscles, trillions of cells, and innumerable atoms. It is coordinated by a brain through a network of nerves which bear striking resemblance to the circuitry of computers. But it is infinitely more compact, miniaturized and unified than any contrivance humans have yet to build—or are likely to build.

May this same miracle find its counterpart in our life together under the administering Spirit of the Lord.

Caring

The Practice

Every pastor needs to be a CPA in terms of skills—not as an accountant, but as this acronym represents Caring, Preaching, and Administration. Any given congregation depends upon ordained clergy to provide leadership in each of these areas. Without administrative capability, the ecclesiastical ship of state drifts. Preaching provides the incomparable focal point of a hurch's common life.

But caring is very intentionally placed first in this sequence :ause it is at the heart of the pastoral relationship. Parishio- s can suffer less than compelling preaching, or can forgive ciencies in keeping the organizational wheels well oiled. But y find it hard to bear with a pastoral leader who is indiffer- to people's practical, emotional, or spiritual needs. So pasto- care must, of necessity, come first in the list of aptitudes :ded in effective ministry.

Definition

TLC—Tender Love and Care—is the operating definition of ring in the larger society today. While inseparable from tender eling, it is nonetheless distinguishable as the practical ression of love.

The on-going issue within the religious community is wh ier to make distinction between the caring done by clergy and that extended by laity. Certainly within the Protestant tradition, with its "priesthood of all believers" conviction, there is no question that the caring of the ordained and of congregational members is of a piece. Any difference is that of function, not of kind.

As one maintains the functional distinction between pastoral care and lay caring, the clergy's particular role may be more clearly perceived. The pastor is unique in terms of caring availability, coordination, and training.

Indeed, there is no more important rationale for the support of full-time clergy than to allow some in the community to be readily available to respond quickly and directly to people's needs. Moreover, that additional margin of energy and time enables some to be in position to pull together the efforts of others in a unified response to those needs. Theological education provides specialized training in caring which finds its fulfillment as these skills are shared with others in the congregation.

Skills

In terms of my own practice, I have found that there is no substitute for calling, counseling, and providing structure and training for laity. Nor is there any doubt that crisis calling will take priority as clergy clearly manifest genuine concern by being readily present to the people they serve in times of emergency.

In all circumstances the caring pastor will have the "sixth sense" to know when silence is as appropriate as speaking. Body language may prove to be more effective than the spoken word.

I recall an instance of spending long hours with a family in an ICU waiting room. The tedium was broken as my suggestion was gratefully taken for the anxious parties to give one another back-rubs, thereby relieving physical and emotional tensions. Indeed a case could be made for a "Church of the Blessed Backrub" in our skin-hungry era.

I have also found that singing to stroke victims communicates in a way that talking doesn't. Because singing draws from the opposite hemisphere of the brain than speaking, sometimes the patient who is not able to say a word can, nevertheless, respond in song.

Calling

But "maintenance calls" are no less important than those in moments of crisis. While doctors may no longer make house calls, pastors certainly need to do so. Seeking to visit each family at home within the first year of a new pastorate is a vital expression of interest and concern.

Following the initial "get-acquainted visit," I continue to drop-in (although almost always preceded by making an appointment) on people periodically. I term these "grace-calls"- i.e. with no other purpose in mind than to see how individuals are doing. While less frequent, visitation at people's place of work has been well received.

But in betwixt and between prearranged visits are the significant pastoral contacts which present themselves in the daily round. When someone joins the church, I provide this list of "Ten Times to Call Your Pastor," as a reminder of the variety of circumstances in which pastoral care is appropriate:

1. When there is illness or hospitalization
2. When there is a death in the family
3. When there is prolonged reaction to grief
4. When family difficulties arise
5. When addiction threatens
6. When spiritually depressed
7. When a "sounding-board" for decision-making is needed
8. When a baby is born
9. When baptisms, weddings need planning
10. When personal/family celebrations of other of life's "passages" need preparing

In response to any of the above, it should be noted that caring is frequently communicated over the phone. In fact, there is a special elicitation of feeling which often comes in this non-face-to-face setting. Audiologists have found that there are three hundred more nerve endings in the ear than in the eye.

The art of writing letters and notes to people is a subject in itself. But let it only be noted that "a little goes a long way," as any number of occasions prompt pastoral attention in the form of hand-written remembrances. Paying such informal heed to individuals is likely to be as healing as that most formalized aspect of caring practices counseling.

Counseling

Yet this perspective in no way minimizes the necessity of effective pastoral counseling. Like many in my generation, I was instructed to employ a modified form of Carl Roger's method of "non-directive" counseling. His emphasis on empathy, as reflecting what another is feeling and attending with "the third ear," remains indispensable for those in the helping professions.

Not only has this approach now been modified by the fitting use of more assertive responses, but also within the faith community other emphases are reasserting themselves. Thomas C. Oden in "Recovering Pastoral Care's Lost Identity," a chapter in Aden and Ellens' *The Church and Pastoral Care*, did a comparative study of 19th and 20th century pastoral theologians.

Those in the last century uniformly cited the work of Augustine, Chrysostum, Gregory the Great, Luther, Calvin and Baxter. Those whose writings were surveyed in this century since the founding of the Clinical Pastoral Education training in the 1920s made no reference to these traditional sources. Rather it is such psychotherapeutic authorities as Freud, Jung, Fromm and Bernre who are cited.

Oden concludes that a synthesis is needed. The models for clergy counseling could and should be related to pastoral life as much as to secular techniques. He rightly observes that doors are opened upon pastoral visitation which remain closed to other therapists. The group process of religious communities, forgiveness/restitution, and spiritual disciplines are among the resources which add incomparable richness to pastoral counseling.

Sharing the Caring

But to add the most to any given ministry the clergy must offer leadership in building a caring team. This leading includes both organizing for caring in terms of developing caring structures and training in caregiving.

A caring committee provides the means of implementing corporate concern. The responsibilities could encompass the development of a call tree, an instrument for insuring that every person in a congregation is in touch with one of its officers. Procedures are in order for dividing the duties in following up on those with blessings or concerns: whether remembrances at a time of birth or arranging for food at a time of death, or in following up on shut-ins. The natural support-groups, whether they be choirs or circles or other fellowships, may be drawn into the process.

It is through this committee that training may be offered for improving caring skills. While some congregations utilize outside caregiving training services, such as the Stephen Ministries, others develop their own grassroots/eclectic programs. Local models are described in Detwiler-Zapp and Dixon's Lay *Caregiving*. But whatever the source of assistance, the elements of caregiving are the same: listening, responding, crisis intervention, referring, and understanding grief.

A final example may help focus this "C" part of the CPA requirements needed by all clergy. It came in the form of an older person who had virtually no family and who could no longer remain in her home. This critical "passage" for her necessitated the intervention of a pastor, who served as the catalyst to bring together others from the church, concerned neighbors, and the one distant cousin. Cooperatively arrangements were made in terms of establishing power-of-attorney and searching to find the fitting nursing home. The pastor also functioned to facilitate the process of transition, both spatially and spiritually.

Social work and pastoral care blend into one another in such instances. Likewise does the collective practice flow naturally into the preaching which illumines its spirit.

The Preaching

CARING-THE HEART OF LOVE

Luke 10:25-37

The story you've just heard is perhaps the most beloved of all that Jesus told. There are pastoral counseling centers throughout the land which take their name from that parable of the Good Samaritan. There are hospitals so named, and even a statute on the book of some states which takes its title from this tale.

Yet familiar as this story is to us, we run the risk of familiarity breeding, if not contempt, at least an assumption that we know all that there is to know about it. Yet like the other teachings of our Lord, we should be prepared for surprises —

at how new depths of meaning continue to present themselves. Let us be led by the questions he raises and by the way he repeats himself.

As for the questions, you may have heard of the one rabbi who asked another rabbi, "Why do you always answer a question with a question?" To this the other replied, "Do I?" Well, that's what Rabbi Jesus does in this story with the rabbinical lawyer - doing so twice.

He does so at the beginning, in answer to the scribe's question about inheriting eternal life. He also does so at the end, in reply to a follow-up question about who is the neighbor to be loved.

In between the beginning and the end, Jesus takes his questioner, and takes us, through a process of discovering how love is at the heart of the Great Commandment and how caring is at the heart of love. It is a process which involves helping us discover answers which are already within ourselves. And the parable of the Good Samaritan, which follows the teaching about the Great Commandment, is not completed until the responsibility is left with the questioner to make that indispensable connection between love and caring.

Compassion

Let us, then, focus upon the caring element in the parable, where Jesus uses that term twice. First, he described how the Samaritan stopped and "took care" of the beaten man lying by the side of the road; and how he later brought the victim to an innkeeper and paid him to "take care" of the man. Consequently as we read between the lines of this story we are led to recognize how love is defined by the elements of caring: love being compassionate, courageous, and inclusive.

Caring begins with compassion. That element is what makes Jesus' teaching so distinctive from that of the Temple system, where the primary virtue was purity. Rather, as Jesus taught elsewhere, "Be compassionate as your Father in heaven is compassionate."

"Compassion" in the Greek literally pertains to the intestines, because the people of that day identified the moving of the viscera with the feeling of emotions. In the Hebrew the term is also associated with the womb. So the compassion, the pity, the nurturing of God is meant to be imitated.

Now that's the starting point for Jesus' portrayal of the Good Samaritan, as distinct from all the attempts to measure out kindness according to persons' deserving. The scribe wants to know who the neighbor is on the assumption that love is limited and must be measured out.

So Jesus went to the heart of the commandment quickly, in parable form, in contrast to the way the religious establishment was forever picking through the law with a fine-toothed comb. The conventional wisdom was that the law contained 613 commandments, with 365 "thou shalt nots" and 248 "thou shalts." For anyone to come along and presume to answer the weightiest of questions, as to how eternal life was to be inherited, how to love God and neighbor without making distinction between the greater and lesser of the commandments —- all this seemed to violate "Robert's Rules of Ecclesiastical Order."

Instead of trying to pick through all these detailed legal descriptions about who is the neighbor meriting love, Jesus simply tells the story of one person taking pity on another, showing compassion, being a caring soul. In doing so, did you notice how he turns the spotlight from the neighbor to the one called to be a caregiver?

Courage

Also did you notice how Jesus ironically implied how the second element of caring, courage, was a missing one when it came to the religious professionals. They were the ones not to care because they were afraid to stop alongside the way where the man had been left for dead.

Just to appreciate the riskiness of the situation, let us recognize what it was for anyone to be "going down from Jerusalem to Jericho." That's a drop of 3000 feet in just fifteen miles. The road between the high and low places descends so abruptly, with so many twists and turns that it was made for muggers, who could ambush passers–by from any number of hiding places. So are we given this picture of the man who had been robbed, beaten, and left in circumstances which would have been hazardous for anyone else.

Now when we are also made to visualize the clergy of the day hurrying by, we can imagine the rationalization which may have come to their mind. To touch a victim who had been so stripped and wounded would have caused a priest to become ceremonially unclean; he would thereby have been disqualified from taking his turn in leading the temple worship for a probationary period.

But the more compelling reason for their having passed by on the other side was undoubtedly their fear. The same bandits who attacked before might be around in the shadows to do so again. Therefore, when the Samaritan was described as the person to show compassion, and bind up the wounds of the one who was bleeding to death, we are meant to understand that his caring was also a daring. It took courage to risk being assaulted himself.

Likewise it takes courage for any of us to care. We hear candidates for public office say that they really care. Yet the measure of genuine concern for the public is whether they are willing to take the political risk of spelling out what it would really take to bind up the nation's wounds, as distinct from pandering to popular prejudice.

By the sound of today's political oratory, you'd think that it was welfare mothers who produced the savings and loans scandals, which bilked the treasury far more than the Aid to Dependent Children program. Moreover, there is precious little attention given to the causes of violence and poverty or concern for what brings about the unsafe places where people are getting waylaid regularly. Such forthrightness is so often rewarded by defeat at the election box. Yet whatever signs of cowardice are evident among public figures, it may reflect the reluctance of each of us to come terms with our own exclusive tendencies.

Inclusiveness

So it is that the third dimension of caring is inclusive love. It's no accident that Jesus portrays the compassionate, courageous caregiver as a Samaritan. When Jesus concluded the parable by answering the question with the question of who proved neighbor to the man, you could almost hear the scribe choking on his words, "The one who showed mercy on him." Samaritans were considered half-breeds by the Jews, bastardized in blood and belief. Thus for the purist scribe to find himself identifying with the outcast provided the surprise ending.

Of all the aspects of caring in Christ, none continues to be more unexpected than this inclusiveness. It is one thing to be compassionate and courageous on behalf of those who are naturally near and dear to us. But what about those we don't even know, particularly if they are not "our kind"? Yet that is what gives Christian love its distinctiveness, even if we have to be reminded of that by outsiders who sometimes resonate to the uniqueness of Jesus even more than some of us who go by his name.

I think of Mohandas Gandhi who as the leader for the independence in India quite clearly invoked the name of Jesus as the one inspiring non-violent movement. That influence of the Lord was further evident on the piece of paper which Gandhi slipped to his grandchild just before his assassination in 1948 and which listed what he called "The Seven Blunders of the World." These included:

Wealth without Work
Pleasure without Conscience
Knowledge without Character
Commerce without Morality
Science without Humanity
Worship without Sacrifice
Politics without Principle

This grandson, now fifty years later, continues the peacemaking efforts of his grandfather and has added his own eighth blunder: Rights without Responsibilities. Speaking recently to high school students in Seattle on Martin Luther King's birthday he noted, "We are always fighting for our rights, but I haven't seen anybody fighting for their responsibilities." So does a Hindu well remind Christians of how caring we are meant to be.

Our Decision

But even after replaying this parable in such a way as to discover what we may not have perceived before, to better discern how the love of God, neighbor, and oneself is inseparable from the caring, composed of these compassionate, courageous, and inclusive elements—even after all that, we are left with an open-ended story. We don't know if the lawyer went out and did as the Samaritan was said to have done. We are left to make our own decision as to whether our caring will be as complete and consistent as Jesus portrayed. So we might as well not conclude until we admit our need for help in being helping.

Yet when we know ourselves to have been so cared for, as Jesus reveals the heavenly Father to be deeply devoted to us, when we feel Christ's courage in going to the Cross for your sake and mine, when we who have felt like outsiders and pariahs have known ourselves to have been included in Christ's Body, then in gratitude we are empowered to become an instrument of a Higher Power.

Let us, therefore, "Go and do likewise" as Jesus encourages us to do. While we cannot be all things to all people, we can be far more than we been. While there may be a limit to what we can do and be to others, there is no limit to the eternal resources of caring from which we draw.

Communications

The Practice

"In the beginning was the word...." It's no accident that communications comes first in John's gospel. Nor is it by happenstance that this text echoes the first verse of the first book of the Hebrew Bible. Creation is inseparable from the communications process.

The Necessity

Anthropologists have identified language as that which gives humanity its distinctiveness. Culture and civilization are of a piece with the capacity to receive and send messages.

Frederick the Great is said to have conducted an experiment in which certain infants were not to be spoken to, but were to have had all other needs met. The aim was to find what language came naturally to the little ones. Of course, no speech came without speaking. Moreover, the children perished. Survival itself, apart from a flourishing existence, depends upon that give-and-take.

In any attempted take-over of a government, the opposition invariably seeks to seize the mass communications system. For whoever is in charge of the information-flow has gone far in controlling the whole.

These examples are the negative way of pointing up the incomparable potency of the word. Positively, the development of communications skills is the ticket for those who would rise above limitation. To name a fear is to harness its destructive effects. William James said, "Expression deepens impression." To learn to express oneself is to bring a new self into being. There are dimensions and principles of communications which are common to all enterprises, but which apply with special significance in the spiritual community.

The Dimensions

Human communication takes written and spoken, verbal and non-verbal, private and public forms. While a newsletter, for instance, may seem a relatively insignificant part of a local congregation's life, it plays a vital role in the whole.

To shut-ins, for instance, the newsletter may be the only regular tie that they may have with the faith community. A letter from the clergy person may serve as a spiritual "lifeline," when the home-bound lack access to public worship. That letter also provides the means for the pastor periodically to convey an overall vision or direction in a form which reaches everyone concurrently. Therefore, a regular, carefully prepared communique from the leader of the fellowship serves a variety of essential functions.

I find it incongruous that seminaries usually make a point of providing instruction on the musical aspect of church life, but omit guidance in the use of graphics. The layout, design, and eye-appeal of a publication does as much to communicate as the content.

Likewise is non-verbal communication even more powerful in its subliminal effects than the spoken word. When concluding a graveside service, for instance, embracing members of the family does far more to signify warmth than simply pronouncing a benediction.

The intimacy of communication within a religious fellowship is like that within a marriage, the very substance of which is defined by a shared understanding which transcends audible messages. That "sixth sense" in counseling applies to the clergy no less than the secular therapist. But to know when and how to use prayer is a peculiarly rich resource for those in a religious calling.

For prayer opens up the feelings in a way which no other discourse is able to achieve. Instead of saying to a parishioner that I will be praying for her or him, I ask what it is that she or he would have me pray for in her or his behalf. Thus does the devotional practice serve in the clarification of feelings and provides the basis for empathetic response. Communication, at this point, passes into communion.

The Principles

Communications Theory has become a discipline in itself. William Schramm in *The Science of Human Communications* has identified its pioneers and those secular institutions which specialize in its theoretical development. Theodore Baehr's *Getting the Word Out* is a recently published guide to communications in congregations. In analyzing "The Foundations of Powerful Communication," he defines the why, who, what, and how of the process in a religious context. John Edward Lantz not only wrote *Speaking in the Church*, but has endowed a chair in the field at Yale Divinity School.

At the local level, I have found it helpful to be intentional about sharing those understandings and skills with as many in the church as possible. For instance, when instructing youth in a confirmation program, I teach the MAD principles of reading scripture in public, whereby "**M**" means reading meaningfully, **A** means audibly, **D** means distinctively.

These guidelines are not limited to the religious setting. But the reading with expression presupposes a conviction which gives color to the tone and variation to the style of speaking. To project, so as to be heard, shows that the speaker cares about his listeners. To pronounce the words clearly, rather than slur them, evidences that one cares about the text and wants the message to be received.

The necessity, dimensions and principles of effective communication are expressed in the following sermon which serves as the application for this particular aspect of parish practice.

The Preaching

COMMUNICATING FAITH

Habakkuk 1:1-4, 2:1-4

It was while riding on a high-speed train that I thought of this text from Habakkuk. It may seem like a strange connection to make—linking this modern-day conveyance with the teachings of a lesser-known prophet in the remote past. But under those circumstances, that verse lept to mind "Write the vision; make it plain...so he may run who reads it."

To be sure, I wasn't running; but I was moving so fast that the billboards posted in the stations along the way sped by so quickly that all I could do was to catch a glimpse of what was being advertised. And each of those signs had one common characteristic—they were all eye-catching, with large print and few words. All were designed so that those passing rapidly by would get the point. For there is simplicity in all good communication. And that truth is the reason we find this element included in this text.

But what is the message, the vision which would be made plain? The answer is contained in this verse: "Behold, he whose soul is not upright in him shall fail, but the righteous shall live by his faith."

The Talmud, that later Jewish interpretation of the Old Testament, considered this teaching so simple and complete that it declared all 613 commandments of Moses had been reduced to this one—"the righteous shall live by his faith." The Apostle Paul built his whole doctrine of "justification by faith" around this text; and Martin Luther followed suit many centuries later.

But if faith is the content of the vision, and simplicity the means of conveying it, we still are left with the question of why such communication is necessary. That is, in fact, the key to communicating faith at any time and place. For it is the need for faith which gives substance to its meaning and which gives urgency to the means of imparting it plainly.

Receptivity

To determine the original motivation we must go back to the the beginning of the text, as the prophet plays the role of skeptic, asking God "The Why Question."

> Why dost thou make me see wrongs
>   and look upon trouble?...
> For the wicked surround the righteous,
>   so justice goes forth perverted.

In other words, this is another one of those places in the Bible where sensitive souls want to know why evil seems to triumph, and why those who are trying to do the right thing are the ones to suffer. The term "theodicy" has been given to such a challenging of God about how unfair life seems to be.

But whatever we call it, it is the question of questions for most people as far as religion is concerned. It is so perplexing that we find it repeatedly raised in the Bible—in the book of Job, in the Psalms, and certainly in the teachings of Jesus. *Why do Bad Things Happen to Good People?* is the way Rabbi Harold Kushner posed the issue in a best-seller of that title.

When it comes to Habakkuk's faith contribution, we would do well to be faithful to the particular form which that concern took for him. It was some 600 years before the time of Christ. Within Judah justice was being perverted. The Chaldeans, the superpower of the day, was initially perceived as executing judgment upon the unrighteous. Yet their barbarism only compounded the problem—for even more innocent people were being made to suffer. So the prophet's challenge to God persists, until he makes a decision to do more than complain. He says:

> I will take my stand to watch,
>   and station myself on the tower,
> and look forth to see what he will say to me,
>   and what he will answer concerning my complaint.

Before proceeding to the answer that was forthcoming, let us simply recognize how receptive the prophet was, and how receptivity is the prerequisite of any effective communication. Habakkuk shows an expectant spirit—ready to watch. He positions himself to gain a wider view—the reason for stationing himself on the tower, and is prepared to enter into dialogue with the Lord—wanting first to hear and then to make his own reply.

Now no one can really identify that tower for sure. Perhaps it was on the pinnacle of the Temple, or on a favorite overlook from which the prophet could rise above immediate impressions and so broaden his horizons. Yet there is no question that his position included prayer, the mood of receptivity and dialogue with the Maker.

Psychologist Robert Ornstein has distinguished between two forms of consciousness—the action mode and the receptive mode. The active is one of logic, control, of talking. The receptive is that of intuition, surrender, and of listening.

Prayer, to be sure, involves our speaking. But what is often overlooked is how it is primarily a listening, an openness to what comes from beyond. It is in learning to listen, to receive what would never be forthcoming otherwise.

Especially is the tendency great to do little but talk when we have felt ourselves treated unfairly by life, or by God. The temptation is to keep on asking "Why me? Why me, Lord?" While the feeling of perplexity is understandable, the fact is that we have a choice of whether to feel sorry for ourselves or not. People may choose to be so immersed in their remorse that all voices are drowned out but their own.

It's been rightly said that the Lord gave us one mouth and two ears that we may do twice as much listening as talking. It was in the listening posture that Habakkuk did indeed receive the inspiration which led to his insight—the vision which he was told to make so plain that people, even on the run, could read it.

Waiting

Before returning to the content of that communique, let us note one other feature of how it comes—both slowly and quickly. The vision "awaits its time...yet hastens to the end." Its coming may seem slow, yet the Lord says to "...wait for it; it will surely come, it will not delay."

If spiritual development seems to come in fits and starts it is because that's the way with growth of any kind. The human race progresses by trial and error—with long stretches of time in which nothing seems to be happening, but then sudden and dramatic breakthroughs occur. It's the way you and I as individuals "make haste slowly."

I know of one coming out a painfully abusive marriage. Her reentry into church life occurred only after she made the most strenuous efforts to screw up her courage to break away from a relationship that had imprisoned her. Every hair was exactly in place as an outward sign of how much she was fighting for control.

So the warmth of genuine Christian fellowship came as a refuge and strength. No one pushed her to tell her story or to "sign on the dotted line." Gradually she began to trust these new friends who helped mid–wife her into the next stage of her life. Today she provides wide–ranging leadership within that ocngregation and the community of whcih she is a part.

Now that is what the storybooks call "a happy ending." But what happens when it doesn't turn out happily?

That reality, which can be denied only if we were to fly in the face of the facts, is what brings us back to the content of the prophet's vision, the substance of the communication about coping with life's apparently unfair treatment. While Habakkuk says that the insight is slow to come, it will, nonetheless, and sometimes with breathtaking speed. Again:

> Behold, he whose soul is not upright...will fail,
> but the righteous shall live by...faith.

The downside of that truth is that those who seem to be getting by with murder, in the end, won't, while the upside is that those with integrity will survive well. This prophet comes to that realization because he is viewing the scene from a tower, in broad perspective.

So on a clear day of prayer, you can see forever, discerning how destructive consequences come upon those who don't tell or do the truth.

So there it is, so plain and simple that even we who run may read—in the name of him who came that we may have life, and have it abundantly.

For it is in the name of him who in the Parable of the Sower provided all the elements of good communication—the broadcasting/sending of the word, the planting/receiving in the soul's good soil.

It is the name of the one who modeled that process, not only in his teaching, but in his life, death, and resurrection. For when God sends the very best, and the world receives the Word in the worst way, the good news is that "the light shines in the darkness, and the darkness has not overcome it."

Therefore let us become those who receive him, who believe in his name, who are given power to become children of God.

Conflict Resolution

The Practice

In the March 1994 issue of the *The Clergy Journal,* G. Lloyd Rediger wrote in his "Managing the Clergy Killer Phenomenon,"

> My column in *The Clergy Journal* ("Clergy Killers" August 1993) brought an outpouring of phone calls, letters, and requests to come speak to clergy groups and conventions. These responses affirm my thesis that CK's are not figments of clergy imagination nor excuses for discouraged pastors to whine.

It so happened that the February 23, 1994, issue of *The Christian Century* carried an article on a similar theme entitled, "Pastors Under Fire: A Personal Report." In it author Michael Smith reported that in the Southern Baptist Convention alone during an eighteen-month period in 1989 some 2100 pastors were fired—a thirty-one per cent increase over the previous five-year period. He contended that what happened in the SBC was a good indication of what is happening in many denominations.

The recurrence of the conflict theme in regard to pastoral relations is an indication of the prevalence of church disputes otherwise. The question then presents itself as to why this phenomenon is of such epidemic proportions.

The Causes

The Alban Institute in Washington D.C. has identified patterns of conflict over its twenty-year history of providing consultation services to local congregations and judicatories. Its founding director Loren Mead has stated that an important cause of this trend is that the social context and definition of the pastor's role is far more unsettled than it was just a generation ago.

What is true with pastors is but a reflection of the larger pattern of contentiousness throughout the whole of society. Within the public education community it has been noted that the average length of tenure of school superintendents is now three years. Long stretches of service in other public offices is becoming more the exception than the rule. "Downsizing" is creating a diminished sense of loyalty in corporate institutions, with a higher level of anxiety, discord, and stress.

In the era of Rush Limbaugh and other such talk show hosts, a negative climate has been created not only in regard to political authority but to all other institutions. In "The End of Dignity," an article in the March 4, 1995, issue of *The New York Times*, columnist David Gelernter writes, "The slow death of dignified public discourse echoes throughout our culture."

The "culture wars" find their expression in the religious community, where the consensus which keeps congregations together is eroding. Within the Presbyterian Church USA the struggle over homosexuality and feminist issues is just one instance of how denominational structures become battle grounds.

But even in seemingly less turbulent times, church conflicts have always abounded. Biblical commentator J. B. Phillips remarked that if one were to have taken the roof off the New Testament Church, strife would have been found to be no less rife. Human nature, yet to be redeemed, results in petty and not-so-petty feuds.

Pastors are in a particularly exposed position to be lightning rods in conflicted situations. Certainly those who take issue with clergy need not be presumed to be "clergy killers." There may well be a legitimate reason for discontent with pastoral leadership in any given case.

Yet whether the disputes be justified or not, conflict resolution becomes increasingly a necessary pastoral skill. Clergy inevitably "get caught in the middle."

Guidelines

Rediger's "survival skills" and Smith's suggestions for coping serve as helpful guidelines, to which I have added, based on my own experience. Clearly the first element of working through differences is not to deny that they exist. As in all other relationships, it is far better to confront the issues rather than to let them fester.

But the way the differences are faced is as important as that they are acknowledged. Certainly it is vital that the leadership of a congregation seek to resolve difficulties before seeking outside intervention. Jesus provided the perfect model for the various stages of working through contention in Matthew 18:15-20. Starting with one-on-one discussion, then bringing in a third party if that step is insufficient, then taking it to the larger community if the previous steps do not avail—that pattern is no less valid today.

Any effort to short-circuit that process should by all means be avoided. Officers and pastors should be especially alert to resist emotional appeals which seek to "bring in the posse" before going through the "in-house" process first. Hasty action to keep people from being upset is an appeasement which in the long run makes matters worse. Molehills do indeed become mountains if that biblical principle is not followed.

If outside intervention becomes necessary, then there are further guidelines which are critical. Well meaning but inadequately trained volunteer interveners may lack the time and skills to do justice to a complex case. Moreover dispute resolution centers or other agencies which provide certified professionals in mediation services may bring a more disinterested presence to negotiations than those provided through denominational structures.

I have also found Kenneth C. Haugk's book *Antagonists in the Church* a particularly important study when it comes to the warning about not going public in order to work out disputes. To bring a whole congregation in on a matter of discord which properly belongs to the church leadership is to create confusion, doubt, and discouragement. The best mediation procedure in any setting is to define the issues very specifically and to be no less specific in identifying the disputing parties.

It is also vital to learn to distinguish between good-faith differences and those which are the result of destructive intent. Those altercations which arise from honest differences of opinion could and should lend themselves to the scriptural mandate for reconciliation. But in the face of intransigence, of persons keeping things stirred up, when forgiveness is not asked for and the words, "I'm sorry" never pass from the lips of a given person or group, then a power struggle is under way, and then there is no substitute for church discipline.

Dysfunction

Within the church the assumption is that those with opposing views or feelings should be able to negotiate differences. That means that the focus in confrontation will be on behavior rather than on personalities, with steps to improve the working relationships being the desired outcome. It is to everyone's interest not to hold ill will toward anyone.

Maintaining a benevolent spirit, however, is a particular challenge when meeting up with malevolent behavior. Whether destructive results are intended or not, dysfunction is an evil which must be candidly identified and dealt with.

One sign of dysfunction occurs when parties talk behind the backs of others—"triangulating" being the cureent term for that age-old malady. Secrecy is another indication of an unhealthy situation, such as when anyone communicates "Don't tell or show this to anyone else." The active recruiting and organizing of dissidents is a sure indication of intended divisiveness. When confrontation comes as a "surprise attack," with written notices of conflict sent out without previous attempts to speak with accused parties directly, then it is more than etiquette which is breached. When polarization occurs, when laity wedge themselves between staff members, when lay people wind up swearing at lay people, when friendships are broken, then evidence of dysfunction abounds.

The fact is that congregations, as volunteer organizations, are extremely fragile, and in today's tumultuous world they are prone to be "sitting ducks" for discordant elements. It's been rightly said that we are increasingly subjected to "vocal rather than local control." Most members of a congregation may be satisfied with the leadership and direction of a church, but might well become victims of a faction which does not "study the peace, unity and purity of the church," as one vow of eldership has it.

In some instances the Judo principle is the most appropriate response, whereby the aggression of another is allowed by its own momentum and weight to fall and thereby lead to its own defeat, with the intention of leaving contending parties whole persons. But it is especially incumbent upon officers of a congregation always to exercise genuine leadership, by not letting hurtful and outrageous charges go unanswered. Finally, Jesus' words about the limits of reconciliation attempts are fitting, when it becomes necessary "to shake the dust from your feet" and move on.

Benefits

No analysis of conflict within the religious community is complete without noticing the potential benefits which may result. When clergy suffer from any kind of "martyr complex," then they are setting themselves up to become victims. So if there be gain in the pain of conflict, then ordained persons will learn that there simply isn't any substitute for assertive pastoral leadership.

Moreover, when finding themselves in the crossfire, clergy should be led to take corrective action where there is room for improvement. They may find themselves drawing from spiritual resources previously taken for granted or left untapped. For the first time ministers may learn to turn for help and support from colleagues and friends and perhaps from counseling services. Both ministers and spouses, who are inevitably impacted, need to reach out and be ministered to.

Handling conflict creatively will also result in beginning to get at the causes of personal and corporate discord. Unresolved griefs, leading to chronic anger and frustration, often displaced on parties not even responsible for the original problem, can be worked through if identified early and treated faithfully. A congregation may indeed be energized at a time of conflict to discover anew its reason for being at a particular place and time.

As the laity of the church begin to "step up to the plate" to take responsibility for their own community, including pastoring the pastor, then the resolution of conflict may contribute to the revolution of consciousness of which the apostle wrote in his letter to the Corinthian church.

The Preaching

RECONCILIATION: A NEW PERSPECTIVE

2 Corinthians 5:16-6:1

You will likely have recognized one portion of this text which is used often in the liturgy of our worship service, "Therefore, if anyone is in Christ, that person is a new creation; the old has passed away; behold, the new has come."

It is this verse which serves as an assurance of pardon, because it comes in association with how "in Christ God was reconciling the world to himself," not counting our trespasses against us."

Such a declaration of forgiveness is indeed very much at the heart of the gospel, because reconciliation implies our having been estranged from and needing to be made at–one with God. To admit that need is no longer to regard others from an old point of view but to become ambassadors of that same reconciliation in the world.

The Need

The situation to which Paul was addressing his letter clearly bespoke that need for reconciliation. Some in the church at Corinth who spoke in tongues were looking down upon others who seemed less "spiritual" than themselves. Because of the emphasis upon spirituality in our age, we should be able to identify with his warning about so passing judgment upon others. For nothing is more subjective than spirituality. What is one person's spiritual food may be another person's pablum.

Certainly in an age of alienation, we should be able to make quick identification of the need to be reconciled in the broadest sense. That estrangement is particularly obvious as we turn on our television sets. As the rich get richer and the poor get poorer across the face of the earth, as the pace of technological change so quickens as to weaken all traditional forms of social control, as the consequences of now-defunct colonial and imperialist regimes play themselves out, then the instances of warfare and "ethnic cleansing" multiply.

Former President and peacemaker Jimmy Carter, whose Carter Center in Atlanta monitors wars around the world, speaks of how conflict has grown since the end of the Cold War. He identifies 100 current conflicts and 32 major wars.

I once heard a Palestinian Christian leader illustrate the tendency to engage in chronic and destructive conflict by telling the age-old story of the frog and the scorpion who found themselves on the shores of the Jordan River, which they both wanted to cross. The scorpion asked the frog for a ride. The frog resisted, saying that if he let the scorpion on his back he feared the passenger would sting him to death.. To this the scorpion replied, "I wouldn't do that because we would then both drown."

Assured by that reasoning, the frog allowed his otherwise mortal enemy upon his back, and they were soon half way across the Jordan. But then, at the deepest part of the river, the scorpion did sting the one bearing him. As both were sinking to their death, the frog cried out, "Why did you do that?" To this the scorpion answered, "It is the Middle East, you know."

As if it were not bad enough to have such endemic hostilities worldwide, we are witnesses to its happening within the church. The controversy over the ordination of gays and lesbians in a number of denominations has left persons feeling alienated from each other, either because they believe traditional values have been forsaken, or because they believe there is no hope in a church which seems so reactionary as to be unwilling to change.

Then, as we come closer to home, we sense how it is possible for any given local church to fall into factions. The same dynamics which make for dysfunctional families have always been at work within congregations. Whether it is a denial of difficulties on the one hand or of a compulsion to stir up trouble on the other, the need for reconciliation is no less compelling locally as it is globally. How do we learn how to "Fight like Christians"?

Fighting like Christians?

The Starting Point

Certainly Paul would have us begin with our own relationship with God. If you feel that God is indifferent or even antagonistic to you, then your relationship to yourself and to others is going to be one of estrangement. So the starting point is that God so cares about you as "not to count your trespasses against you."

Over the years, the more I've thought about how we move beyond admitting our need for reconciliation to accessing the power of God, the more I'm convinced that it has to do with our point of view. An example of the difference perspective makes in the process comes in the form of a story of two people who each wanted the same orange. A third party who was playing a mediating role was tempted at first to resort to the conventional method of taking a knife and cutting the fruit in half. But this solution was going to leave both sides unhappy.

As it happened, the difference was resolved when it was learned that each side was wanting something different from the orange. One person was desiring the fruit on the inside; the other was interested only the peel on the outside. Once the respective interests were identified, then cooperation replaced confrontation. So does that truth-in-fiction story reflect the means of reconciliation by looking at an issue or a person from a different point of view.

So it is with our spiritual perceptions. Such a shift in perspective is what Paul speaks of in regarding no one any longer from a "human point of view." For Paul that change in outlook occurred as he ceased perceiving Jesus as the anti-Christ, whose followers he was meant to persecute. Rather, he was led on the road to Damascus to behold Jesus as none other than the Christ himself. From that point on he led persons of all future generations to begin viewing each other differently.

It was on a medieval highway in Europe where a learned Renaissance scholar was waylaid by robbers and left for dead. When picked up by authorities and taken to doctors for treatment, he was so beaten up that they took him for a vagrant, a ne'er-do-well who had brought the affliction upon himself. So they spoke in Latin to one another, as they were sure he could not understand them, "Why should we trouble ourselves to treat this worthless creature?" To this they were startled to hear the victim declare, also in Latin, "You dare call worthless one for whom Christ did not disdain to die?"

It is discerning our infinite worth which will serve as motivation for our ceasing to feel at odds with God, our neighbors and ourselves. The new creation precedes and is followed by a new perspective from the Cross where Christ did not disdain to die for you and me.

Two-Way Process

Ultimately reconciliation is a two-way process between persons which will be made complete as one becomes an ambassador of that reconciliation with others. It's that cooperative effort which the apostle is urging upon us to be "...working together with him" in the ministry of reconciliation.

Such ministry does not preclude facing up to conflict. Nor does it imply that anyone should be a doormat for others to walk all over. But it does mean that tension need not become destructive, that ultimately the differences which divide us can be dealt with constructively.

An instance of Christians demonstrating the meaning of the original Greek word for reconciliation, "*katallassein,*" meaning "to change," was the prayer written for the General Assembly of the Presbyterian Church USA following the much publicized RE-imagining Conference. The controversy surrounding the issue of "*sophia,*" the feminist image of God, even made *The McNeil-Lehrer News Hour* and Ted Koppel's *Nightline*.

The prayer, following the lengthy hearings on the subject, expressed the truth that without a willingness to change on all sides, save God's side, there could be no peace. So the forgiveness sought in the prayer was confession of how those on the various sides of the issue had been party to hurting others by denying their concerns, had been party to hurting others by bringing the integrity and intentions of others into question, had been party to attempting to silence or marginalize others. The "sweet gift of reconciliation" was sought "by which apologizes might be offered and accepted, and understanding and forbearance might be practiced." Healing was sought so "all may cease and desist from whatever prevents us from getting on with the mission of the church."

Indeed, this prayer does move us in the direction of regarding "no one from a human point of view." May each of us and all of us together become "a new creation" in Jesus Christ.

Education

The Practice

A number of years ago, I took the age-old melody of "Are You Sleeping, Brother John?" and put new words to it. The new lyrics go like this:

> The church is praying,
> The church is teaching,
> And serving too, serving too.
> Praying, teaching, serving,
> Praying, teaching, serving,
> Allelu! Allelu!

The reason for this adaptation was to help children learn the purpose of the church in a simple and memorable way. For worship, education, and mission is the threefold goal of any congregation, whatever the local variation may be.

And of the "big three," education is one that deserves special treatment in an age of declining Sunday school attendance, as well of participation in other religious nurture programs. Therefore, it is well to be clear about just how vital is the learning/teaching process to the church's mandate.

Didaché Imperative

The starting point has to be a dedication to what in the Greek New Testament is termed *didaché*. In *The Teaching Minister*, Clark

M. Williamson and Ronald J. Allen survey the church education field and make this point at the beginning of their 1992 study: "Teaching the faith has always been inseparable from proclaiming it; *didaché* is as necessary as *kerygma*."The authors then proceed to show how everything teaches in the ministry and in the church.

To be sure there is a temptation to take any one aspect of ministry and make it the prism through which all else in the religious community is run. It was once fashionable to say "The church is mission." The truth is that viewed from various perspectives, the church can be seen in terms of each of its unifying functions.

Yet education serves an indispensable function in regard to those contexts defined by the studies reported in *Contemporary Approaches to Christian Education* (edited by Jack C. Seymore and Donald E. Miller in 1982), having to do with the Faith Community, Faith Development, and Faith Interpretation.

Faith Community Context

"Religion is caught more than it is taught." This aphorism does indeed catch the way in which faith is communal—a reality often overlooked in our hyper-individualistic age. Faith is not only caught but finds its expression in relationships.

A practical result of that insight for me was to lead in establishing a program simply called Mid-Week in a congregation made up primarily of younger families. Inspired by Wesner Fallaw's *Church Education for Tomorrow*, I launched what proved to be a seventeen-year undertaking, in which junior highs gathered for Wednesday night dinner, and a multi-dimensional two-year confirmation program. The two-hour time frame afforded more opportunity for more in-depth Bible study, church history, and worship emphasis than was possible in a Sunday morning format. Moreover, there was opportunity to include drama, music, and graphic arts as community-building activities. Years after the experience, former students-become-adults would recall how that set of experiences was like osmosis in terms of absorbing faith beyond the particular knowledge and skills acquired.

They witnessed to how confirmation was not experienced as an end, but as the beginning of a growth process.

In the congregation I currently serve, the long-time tradition of an intergenerational Wednesday Night Dinner serves a comparable purpose. Weekend retreats or camp experience provides the fellowship, the *koinonia,* within which *didaché* take on personal dimension.

Faith Development Context

"From the cradle to the grave" is the time span within which faith development occurs. Horace Bushell in *Christian Nurture* contended that it is well when a child grows up in a home never knowing anything but that he or she is a Christian.

Yet whether immersed in such nurturing environment or not, all have faith decisions to make in "the stages along life's way." Developing a list of learning objectives for each age level with the local church is an important corporate exercise, so as not to be using published material passively.

"Growing older gracefully" becomes the challenge until the end of life. As one wit put it, "Not only can you teach an old dog new tricks. Often there are tricks that only an old dog can learn!" Inevitably as faith is applied to the issues of work and play, to personal fulfillment and public ethics, ultimately to grief and death, Paul's admonition to "put away childish things" becomes compelling. Yet at every stage of its development, faith continues to unfold in terms of interpretation.

Faith Interpretation Context

As its initial definition I find it helpful to present faith as perception. For perception is a way of seeing, thereby refuting the notion that "faith is blind." The example I use is that of a triangular figure, a form which appears at first sight to be composed only of three interior triangles.

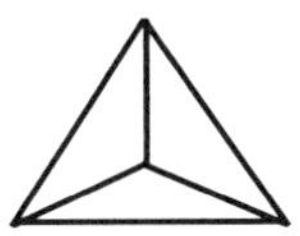

When viewed only two-dimensionally, such is the case. But when perceived as a pyramid from above or to the side as if in an airplane, or from below as if from a mummy's eye view, several other figures present themselves.

So is faith shown to be a creative means of interpreting the world around and within us. Similarly was the revelation to Peter confirmed as he saw past outward appearances to the identity of Jesus as God's transparency.

I have found it helpful to provide a booklet which I wrote entitled, "Seeing the Forest," which is often missed for all the trees of disconnected bits and pieces. A time line of the Bible story, another of the life of Jesus and a third of the story of the church gives an "aerial view" of the whole—a gestalt. (See Appendix.)

Yet there is no substitute for the development of faith as trust. As an infant instinctively and surely trusts an earthly parent, so is a person of any age meant to trust the Heavenly Parent. As the trust-factor is inseparable from keeping a family together and is a prerequisite in doing business together, so is faith in God measured daily by how we cope with our anxieties and by the risks we are willing to take in the name of the one who is forever leading us out.

The Practice

LEADING OUT

Matthew 3:13-17

This story of Jesus' baptism represents the beginning of our education. For as the Lord's baptism marked the start of his ministry, so does our baptism signify a nurturing process which commences with God's cleansing grace.

Teaching/Learning

I can remember when I began the study of Latin, back in the days when they were regularly teaching the subject, that my teacher well illustrated the use of this ancient language. She cited the number of English words which had their origin in Latin, and the first of these that she brought to our attention was "education." Literally meaning "leading out"—"ed + ucare"—she spoke of how that teaching was for the purpose of leading people out of the darkness of ignorance into the light of knowledge.

However, her favorite way of precautioning us that it took learning as well as a teaching for education to happen was to quote a variation of the old adage that you can lead a horse to water, but you can't make it drink. Her version of it was, "You can lead a student to school, but you can't make him think." So there has to be motivation to learn as well as skill in teaching.

Now it happens that there is a built-in image of this reciprocal process in the account of Jesus' baptism, as he is willing to be immersed, and it as he came out of the water—led out in that sense—that the heavens opened with the disclosure of his identity. His teachability and the Spirit's revelation include the same elements which enters into your Christian education and mine.

The Master Teacher

Matthew, the author of the teaching gospel, also shows Jesus as the Master Teacher. For with the Beatitudes as the introduction to that five-part set of teachings called The Sermon on the Mount, and with the Sermon on the Mount as the first of five sets of teaching in the gospel, we are given the perfect example of well-organized instruction.

And why is it that our Lord would start out with happiness as the starting point of becoming a disciple, a learner? Why would he except that Jesus seems to be practicing good psychology, enticing his listeners with a subject which would appeal to them the most.

It's what Sigmund Freud identified as a universal trait, "The Pleasure Principle." It seems that we all want to maximize life's enjoyments and minimize its pains. In a world of Super Bowls, Disneylands, and Pleasure Palaces we are people who spend vast amounts of time and money seeking to amuse ourselves.

Yet when we look more closely at what Jesus says makes for happiness, then we have to wonder whether he's not practicing reverse psychology. For in each of the Beatitudes he speaks of what seems like the opposite of happiness—poverty, grieving, hunger, even persecution.

These paradoxes for the Christian, of course, are examples of how we must come to expect the unexpected from the one we call Lord and Savior. If he really was and is the Son of God, the one whose "ways are not our ways and whose thoughts are not our thoughts," then his teaching will not coincide with the world's definition of happiness.

The Modern Setting

It is the need for that growth process which presents itself to us at this time and place. There is considerable evidence that we are entering into a new Dark Ages when it comes to biblical illiteracy in our society, no doubt part of the overall decline in the preservation of our cultural heritage.

A parishioner of the church once told me of a conversation he had with fellow employees in a local retail establishment. Just for curiosity's sake he posed the question as to how many could name the Ten Commandments. It turned out that no one could name more than two or three of them.

To be sure, there is no guarantee of spiritual prowess in just being able to quote chapter and verse by memory. Yet without having a certain amount of biblical data in mind, there's little chance of having the mind of Christ formed in us. If the teaching of Jesus fundamentally is a closed book gathering dust on our book shelves, then the odds are that our mind-set is being formed by other influences.

Creativity in our teaching ministry with one another must also take into account the electronic revolution that has occurred within the last generation. Neil Postman, who is the most prophetic voice in the field of media, has entitled a book *Amusing Ourselves to Death*. He speaks of television as a driving force to make everything amusing. If left unchecked that compulsion to worship at the altar of amusement is death. Not to take seriously the economic disparities of our nation, much less to ignore how our planet is at risk, is to allow ourselves to be lulled into lethal complacency. For young people, or older folks for that matter, to expect to be entertained constantly when it comes to the religious education within the congregation and within the home environment is to compound our personal and corporate problems.

Close to Home

We are, for instance, accustomed to saying that "Charity begins at home." That is also true in regard to the leading out of Christian nurture. While parents of children may think that they are the cheerleaders on the sidelines rooting for the educators in the church to do their job on the field of teaching young ones their Bible, theology and ethics, it is the church which is meant to provide the support for the spiritual action which truly takes place everyday on the playing field where the family spends most of its time. Therefore, the old adage that "Faith is caught more than taught" always holds true. So was it that Jesus placed special emphasis upon the power of example, teaching, "Let your light so shine before others that they may see your good works and give glory to your Father in heaven."

I am reminded of the mountain man whose job it was to respond to calls for help for those who got stranded in winter storms. One night on one of his outings, he was startled to hear behind him the voice of his son who had unbeknownst to him followed into the darkness and snow. The little one said, "Be careful where you step, Daddy. I'm walking in your tracks."

For any of us who are parents, that is a sobering reminder that we are always being watched. Likewise those who are older brothers and sisters need to remember that subconscious bonding is happening all of the time, and whether it be for good or ill depends upon the example you set.

Martin Luther became a far more caring parent as he struggled beyond the limitations of his own upbringing. His father had been overly strict on him, to the point of being cruel. So Luther was later to say, "Spare the rod and spoil the child is less helpful practice than keeping an apple on hand to give to the child when the little one does well."

So also did the distinguished artist Benjamin West bear witness to how the daily atmosphere in his home as a child was the primary influence in leading him toward later achievement. The experience he recalled with particular vividness was the day his mother stepped out of the house, leaving him, as the older child, in charge of his little sister Sally. In his mother's absence he discovered some bottles of colored ink and began to paint a picture of Sally. In doing so he made a considerable mess.

His mother came back, saw the mess, but said nothing. She simply started to pick things up, before catching a glance at the drawing. "Why," she said, "it's Sally!" She then stooped to kiss him. Ever after Benjamin West used to say "My mother's kiss made me a painter!"

That graciousness truly reflects the Spirit of the God, whose Son now bids us as leaders and followers, disciples and learners all, to be bringing up one another "in the nurture and admonition of the Lord."

FELLOWSHIP

The Practice

We begin with the case of the church which turned its pews around. When undertaking a remodeling project of an entire plant, the leaders decided to reverse the position of the chancel area, so that the seating arrangement was altered correspondingly. What once faced south was then made to face north. But why this change?

The mystery is solved when discovering that a whole new fellowship area was being constructed to serve as the point of entry into the sanctuary, in which the front thereby became the back to accommodate the arrival of worshippers. Thus the fellowship hall came to serve as the spatial center of that religious community. That vestibule, so enlarged as to accommodate all who might choose to remain afterwards for refreshments, had been given such priority that the whole architectural plan pivoted around it.

Is that rearrangement of the sanctuary to accommodate a social gathering place an instance of putting the ecclesiastical cart before the horse? The initial impulse is to answer "Yes!"

But a good theological case, as well as sociological one, can be made for that floor plan. In today's IBM (I've Been Moved) world, the need for roots is deep and abiding. The conversation over a coffee cup following worship may become as sacramental in its own way as passing the cup at the Lord's Supper.

Risks

None of this is to say that the emphasis upon fellowship comes without risks. Not the least of these is that if such visitation remains at the chit-chat level, then its participants are left more lonely than before.

Another clear warning needs to be sounded in regard to the tendency to mix only with "your own kind." Cliques easily develop simply because it's comfortable to gravitate to familiar faces. The church is no less prone to this exclusiveness than are secular groupings.

Yet for all the hazards which come from socializing in congregational life, there is no avoiding the mandate of fellowship. The Judeo-Christian faith is predicated on a communal principle. This fundamental basis was given expression by Philo, the Jewish philospher, who described the relationship between God and Moses as *koinonia*. This intimate face-to-face communion, in turn, served as the spiritual heart of the covenant established between the Lord and Israel.

The Christian tradition continued that same sense of belonging through believers' relationship in Christ. "God is faithful; by him you were called into the fellowship of his Son, Jesus Christ our Lod" (1 Cor. 1:9). That one-to-one sharing finds both its origin and fulfillment in outreach, in extending "the right hand of fellowship."

Handles

In the contemporary world "handle" is also an appropriate term. In our mobile society the issue becomes how to give people a ready–made way to meet, by which communication is facilitated, both initially and on an on-going basis.

The Twelve Step programs offer a model of how quickly and deeply contact may be made as locations and occasions are regularly and almost universally provided. For persons suffering addictive behavior, these support groups come as close to the Communion of Saints as is apt to be experienced on earth.

But other than such instant community available to those coping with compulsions, the communities of faith will want to be intentional and systematic about the fellowship opportunities which they afford for all whom they serve.

I must admit to having had to find my own way in the thicket of these needs. Seminaries seldom include training on how to help folks mix and mingle, much less identify the urgency of that task. Rather my generation of "theologs" was only warned not to let the church become a glorified "Newcomers Club."

But it didn't take long out in the "real world" to discover how group-building is in many ways the name of the game. The turn-around for me was not in switching pews, but in switching priorities. I evolved from something of a "bookworm," thinking that thinking was going to solve the world's problems, to becoming a reader of people. Particularly did that transformation occur as I rather reluctantly found myself accepting the directorship of a summer family camp.

It was in the process of "letting their hair down" through the informality of re-creation that people found that they could be themselves and so open-up as never before. It seemed incongruous, but some of the deepest self-disclosure came in the wake of a volleyball game (apart from who was on the winning or losing side). The bonding which occurred during a week apart provided impetus for the rest of the year, not only for the participating families, but for the whole congregation.

Back on the homefront of weekly/daily programming, it became increasingly apparent to me that a congregation is indeed a group meant to be made up of groups. Church growth, whether viewed numerically or qualitatively, depends on there being a variety of fellowship groups.

Joy

The regular groupings certainly may be perceived as built-in occasions for personal and corporate sharing. The choir, Sunday School classes, circles, even boards and committees can serve as vehicles for partnership in the Spirit. Mission projects represent the way in which fellowship more often than not comes as a by-product of doing the church's work otherwise.

Yet in this "chicken or egg" world, fellowship may precede and serve as cause of worship, education and mission. People's entry into the church may come through a "Fun-Bunch" or a "Mixminsters" as adult fellowships have been variously called in congregations I have served. The needs of particular age-levels may be specifically addressed, as a "20-30 Something" group was formed in what had previously been a church made largely of elderly members.

To that extent we are never to minimize the importance of having fun together in the community of faith. To be sure, such activities may become trivialized. But "God Rest Ye Merry," is for more than for gentlemen and for more than the Christmas season.

As one who plays just enough jazz and pop music to sit down to "tickle the ivories" when people gather informally, I've discovered that the sound level of conversation automatically rises when music begins. Implicit permission is given to relax and to be more forthcoming.

I have also kidded my congregation that after retirement I will play piano bar so as to be able to hear some real confessions! Even now I find people opening up as ballads free them to sing or to reminisce.

It has often been noted how the enjoyment of summer camp experiences has led to serious commitments. For generations people have met marital partners through religious communities where common values are shared.

So we ought not to minimize the turn-arounds which prove possible through the fellowship dimension of religious life. Certainly as a social animal every human being has communal needs and associates on that basis. But within biblically-inspired communities that need takes on a unique and indispensable form.

The Preaching

SIGNS OF FELLOWSHIP

Acts 2:39-47

It happens that the very end of this text marks the beginning of the Church Growth movement. "And the Lord added to their number day by day those who were being saved."

As we seek to unravel the mystery of that Pentecostal outpouring, we will discover one of the essential clues is fellowship. That is the set of relationships listed in the series of activities which followed Peter's preaching, as the people "...devoted themselves to the apostle's teaching and fellowship, to the breaking of bread and the prayers." Somehow fellowship has from the beginning been inseparable from the worship, nurture, and mission of the church.

Definition

Now we might do well to focus first on that Greek word—*koinonia* which is at the root of what we have translated as "fellowship." It's easy to see that our English term for "coin" has the same origin, in each case meaning what is held in common. In Acts that emphasis is evident as those "who believed were together and had all things in common." Such sharing of material possessions was the outward expression of that inward commonality of faith.

Likewise the repeated references to these early believers eating together was still another sign of fellowship. Twice is it mentioned that there was "breaking of bread," including how this was done in homes.

What makes this initial surge of membership even more significant was that the three thousand souls who were originally brought together by the Spirit didn't even speak the same language. It was the multitude who gathered from all lands for the Pentecost festival who became the first Christians. The upshot of such diversity is that fellowship means more than being a religious country club where everyone is of the same race and class.

Even making friends of our enemies, those who exclude us, is indeed a radical departure from the usual way of thinking and relating. That insight accounted for a Christian cooperative in Americus, Georgia naming itself Koinonia Farms. The racial integration practiced there during the days of legal segregation brought persecution. Yet out of that witness arose everything from *The Cotton Patch Gospel* to Habitat for Humanity.

So as we further explore the signs of fellowship in our midst, let us first appreciate just how rare, challenging and creative a reality *koinonia* really is. Let us recognize how as a partnership, community arises both as a gift of God and as result of devoted effort. When we conclude our worship with the benediction which speaks of the "communion of the Holy Spirit," it should be with the understanding that we participate in that "...fellowship of kindred minds which is like to that above."

Communion

So in returning to the first of the signs we will note how the breaking of bread is associated with the sacrament of The Lord's Supper. But let's also recognize how the everyday act of eating can become sacramental.

I learned this truth in a compelling way from a Maryknoll missionary who has been on assignment in the New Territories of Hong Kong. That particular population center has burgeoned with those who are fleeing from the mainland. His parish in a high rise district includes 25,000 people within in a five block radius!

Only a small fraction of them are Christian. But the dislocation of persons from their family roots has broken traditional clannish patterns and has made for a receptiveness to seeing neighbors as extended family. In response to their loneliness, this priest has led these persons to do what they had have never done before—to go into one another's homes for Bible study and to break bread together. He says, "I have borrowed the Protestant's secret weapon—the potluck supper!"

This simple practice of eating together has been essential to demonstrating that *koinonia* is distinct from tight-knit family ties. Desirable and necessary as these natural relationships are, they are not to be confused with that inclusive community to which we are called as Christians.

Sharing

Likewise does the second sign of *koinonia*, the sharing of our material possessions, come as a challenge to the conventional wisdom. Many have taken offense at what seems like communist teaching in the Bible. When we read that those who believed "...would sell their possessions and goods and distribute the proceeds to all who had need," it seems uncomfortably close to the Marxist teaching "from each according to his ability to each according to his need."

Of course, the scripture is not prescribing an economic system, but is simply reporting how enthusiastically people responded to an outpouring of the Spirit. Yet it is that same impetus which continues to impact us materially.

Close to home there are day laborers who gather each morning at a particular intersection hoping for employers to come by and take them to a job waiting to be done. If you drive past, you know it's not a very pretty sight. People lock their automobile doors lest any of the undesirable-looking types might try to force entry.

But each morning at dawn there is a group who comes with hot-coffee and hard-boiled eggs to feed those who are waiting for work. I spoke with one of those who exercises this ministry. The origin for the mission arose from Dorothy Day, who launched The Catholic Worker movement earlier in the century. Locally that ministry has evolved into these errands of mercy.

These caregivers testify to the sincerity of those who brave the elements to show their desire to work, to the capability, warmth and even humor of those waiting on the corner each day. One particular individual is missing a hand, which has been replaced with a hook, which he uses to hammer nails as he places pictures on walls!

Hospitality

So as all Christian believers break bread with those who seem quite unlike themselves, according dignity to those who are so often treated as non-persons, we come to the final sign of fellowship—joyful hospitality. Originally, this element was expressed in terms of persons sharing together "...with glad and generous hearts."

Practicing hospitality is a recurring theme in scripture, and there can be no more compelling evidence of a church alive with the Spirit than in graciously welcoming others to our fellowship. In Hebrews we are enjoined, "Do not neglect to show hospitality

to strangers, for thereby some have entertained angels unawares."

In an era of practicing "benign neglect" (and often not so benign) with others who are "not our kind," the call to be inclusive is particularly challenging. Yet the mandate of the gospel to reach out is clear.

Certainly it is incumbent upon your pastor to be a "heavenly host" when it comes to helping guests feel at home. But each of you is meant to be no less a part of a hospitable congregation. The art of hospitality involves remembering names which is more of a skill than an aptitude. It involves combining a warm welcome with a respect for the privacy of others coming into our midst.

So is it that fellowship—the *koinonia* of communion, sharing and hospitality—is a gift of God, to which we must also bring our best efforts. Any human community is like two logs which burn better than one—and three even better yet, as surface area is increased several times over. But where "two or three are gathered together" in the Lord's name, we can expect a special synergy, as Christ is indeed in our midst.

Funerals

The Practice

The starting point for practicing ministry at the time of death in a congregation is with a policy statement from its governing board. While such official action may seem a rather impersonal way to begin considering this most sensitive of matters, such guidelines provide the necessary framework for faithful pastoral support. The following are those I have used in serving churches over several decades.

The Framework

1. Because of the difficulty of making decisions in a time of distress, members of the congregation are encouraged to make advance arrangements for the funeral. Such plans include provision for disposition of the remains—whether by burial, cremation, or donations for medical purposes. Memorial societies provide information as to less costly alternatives. A copy of written plans may be kept on file at the church office.
2. When death is imminent, the pastor stands with the physician in serving as a resource to the family. He or she is prepared to counsel with the family on funeral arrangements consistent with individual needs and the insights of faith. Such service includes the availability of the pastor in

accompanying the family to a funeral home when arrangements are being made.

3. Members are encouraged to hold funeral or memorial services in the sanctuary as a witness to the resurrection. If there is a casket and it is at the site of the funeral, then its final closing before the service begins is recommended. Any fraternal, civic, or military rite should be conducted separately, prior to the religious service.
4. The service appropriately includes hymns, scripture, a meditation, prayers of thanksgiving, supplication and intercession. Participation by family members, members of the church and friends is welcome, with their contributions coordinated by the pastor.
5. An increasing number of families are choosing to have the committal service conducted first, with only the immediate family present. A memorial service fittingly follows, with an evening hour allowing more persons to attend. A reception, which may substitute for a visitation at the funeral home, can then be provided in the fellowship hall of the church where refreshments may be served. Such a gathering best allows for expression of support by the congregation.
6. The pastor extends services at the time of death to members without honorarium. The church facility is available without cost to the membership. An honorarium is appropriately offered to the organist and soloist. Contributions may be made to the church's memorial fund as a remembrance or in lieu of flowers.

Pastoral Support

All of the above suggestions are toward the end of providing faithful support to the bereaved by both pastor and congregation. Moreover, the pastor's sensitivity and skills in such a critical time must be viewed in the context of his or her broader practice. Except in instances of sudden death, the pastor is likely to have been in ongoing communication with terminally ill individuals and their families. Therefore, the grieving is likely to have begun before death occurs.

Among the most helpful published resources to be shared within this setting is Granger Westberg's *Good Grief*. A more recent book which has gained widespread use is Nicholas Wolterstorff's *Lament for a Son*. Hospice is certainly among the most beneficial of the supportive services to which the pastor may refer families.

The visit with the survivors to plan the service represents an especially creative moment. As the pastor is able to draw forth from family and friends that which each one wants to have included in the meditation, the opportunity is simultaneously present for grieving persons to express the range and depth of their feelings. In addition, various family members are often put in touch with each other as result of that corporate sharing in a way which may not be possible otherwise.

Therefore, the call before the funeral serves as an important catalyst. The following homiletical reflection lifts up other elements implicit in this critical aspect of parish practice.

The Preaching

THE LIFE AFTER

Genesis 49:28-12

The very last verse of this text describes the view of the lifeafter of much of the Old Testament. The scripture simply states "After he had buried his father, Joseph returned to Egypt with his brothers..." In other words, the life after death is for the living. There is virtually nothing about the hereafter for those who have gone before.

As time went along, there did emerge a belief in Sheol, a nether region to which all the dead descended as a mere shadow of their former selves, much like the idea of Hades in Greece. Even when the idea of a resurrection from the dead evolved, within a century or two before the time of Christ, there was no unanimity of conviction about it among the Jews. The Saduccees were a group who persisted in the view that there was no resurrection.

To this day, the Orthodox Jews hold to what we might call a minimalist view of the hereafter.

Now I draw your attention to this particular incident in the Old Testament because it brings us to a great divide. For how we feel and deal with the afterlife is inseparable from other considerations—where we find the strength of our will to live in the face of adversity and how we are enabled to be renewed throughout our life cycle.

Moreover, this early picture of the disposition of the remains of Jacob, and of Joseph getting on with the business of living helps us to gain perspective both on the outer and inner sides of the life after. The outer side has to do with funeral practices—the rituals by which people make this critical passage in life. The inner side has to do with our own dying through grief and rebirth through resurrection faith.

The Outer Side

As we begin with this death in the patriarchal family, we find what was common practice at the time. Jacob wished to be taken back to Cannan, to the family burial plot which had been purchased two generations before, where his grandparents Abraham and Sarah had been buried; where his parents Isaac and Rebekah had been interred; and where his beloved wife Rachel had been laid to rest. "To be gathered to my people," meant for a him a proximity to the physical remains of his forebears.

Yet the mobility of the modern age is changing traditional patterns. What was home to one generation is not likely to be to the next. Moreover, the escalating and often exorbitant costs of funerals has led an increasing number of people into alternative forms of disposition.

Jessica Mitford in her book, *The American Way of Death*, shows how our burial patterns are of relatively recent origin. Embalming, which was possible in Egypt because of the land's aridity, was not practiced again until the time of the American Civil War. A former medical student then devised the preservative technique by which the bodies of Union casualties might be returned to their families elsewhere in the nation. The modern funeral industry has emerged from that beginning just over a century ago.

In recent years memorial societies have arisen to guide individuals and families concerning the options at the time of death. It is not necessary in the midst of confusion or from a sense of guilt to pay costly sums to honor the deceased. Cremation is an ecologically responsible means of disposing of physical remains and is theologically acceptable to many major faiths in the land.

Moreover, organ donation is being increasingly accepted as a valid response of faith. There are at any given time 35,000 blind persons whose sight could be restored through cornea transplants.

These differences in last rites, while representing an outer change from the way Joseph arranged for the burial of Jacob, do not depart from the inner meaning of what was represented in that family. For what is the essence of being "gathered together" with our forebears? Is it not what we call the "Communion of Saints"? Do we not do honor to those who have gone before when the emphasis is upon sharing the same spirit rather than the same space with those we have loved?

I vividly recall visiting my wife's great aunt who lived in Pittsburgh, Pennsylvania. Soon after our arrival she took us on a tour of several of the numerous cemeteries in that city. She was eager to point out the tombstones of a number of family members, the location of which she was the only one left to remember. There was a poignancy in going from one to the other, knowing that the day was not far distant when no one would recognize the names on those markers.

I returned to Pittsburgh a year later to participate in her funeral. At her interment I expressed to the gathering of mostly friends and neighbors that it was this woman's lively spirit and active concern for others which would endure. For at the age of ninety two she had been the one vigorous enough to do the driving for her younger friends—in their seventies and eighties!

Her vitality suggests why the symbol for Christians is not a grave marker, to which the faithful make pilgrimage, but an empty tomb. The released power of Easter is the ultimate resource available to those who are coming to terms with the inner side of the life after—through grief and renewal.

The Inner Side

This second aspect is suggested by the scriptural account of a death in the family—when it records that "Joseph fell on his father's face and wept over him..." Then the text speaks of the "days of weeping" having passed.

Just this much of a description is enough to indicate the inward rhythm of the bereavement process. While the length of time for healing to occur will vary with each individual, and with each set of circumstances, the stages of grief always include a numbness, a subsequent sorting out the pieces, before putting one's life back together again, at least over a year's period.

The initial shock is especially acute in the case of sudden or premature deaths. Cecil Murphy in his helpful book, *Comforting Those Who Grieve,* recounts the experience of a wife who lost her husband in a construction accident. For the first two months there was little sign of grief. Then one morning, as she was sipping her coffee, she caught herself saying, "Harry, would you like to join me?"

When she realized what she had said, still holding her cup in her hand, she walked two blocks down the street into the house of her best friend. Without knocking, she walked past her startled friend, pausing only long enough to put the coffee down, proceeded into the guest room, closed the door, wept, then slept for hours. When she later appeared, she simply said to her friend, "Harry's not coming back, is he?"

In other instances where suffering has been prolonged, and death comes as a merciful blessing, then the disbelief may not be so pronounced. Yet, there is always an incongruity, caused by the continuing presence of the deceased in the heart of the mourner, while no longer being physically present. The pain of grief arises from that contradiction, the tension between emotional presence and bodily absence.

The Lord, in his mercy, has so made us that we do not have to bear that wrench of separation all at once. The tears ebb and flow, as the hurt, triggered by an object or a remark about the deceased, is followed by an easing of the pain.

Likewise, the Lord, in his mercy, has provided the means by which we can cope with the middle-stage of our mourning, which often means coming to terms with guilt. How often there is the lament, "If only..." Often that guilt is groundless. "If only I had visited more often!", when, in fact, the number of visits would have made no difference.

There are other occasions when the basis for guilt is real enough, as with one husband who ignored the wife's complaints until it was too late, with the doctor pronouncing the verdict, "If only you had come to me three months earlier."

In neither case is it helpful to assure the grieving person by saying, "You don't need to feel guilty." In both cases, it is helpful to reflect those feelings, because forgiveness comes only after the guiltless person awakens to the truth of innocence within himself or herself, and only after the guilty party accepts responsibility and forgiveness.

As to religious assurances, these are most often not what is needed. The mother of a child lost in a crib death cried, "Why would God allow such a thing to happen?" To this a chaplain well responded, "You feel confused, angry, and you hurt badly." To this she said, "Yes, more badly than I could ever say." That chaplain wisely perceived that it was not a theological explanation which was being sought, but someone who showed care and understanding.

Nor will we find ourselves saying, "It must have been God's will." As James Agee shows in his story, *A Death in the Family,* where a husband and father dies from a freakish accident—a cotter pin breaking in the steering wheel of a fast moving vehicle—there is no denying happenstance in this universe. One must have the freedom to express anger toward God, if one is eventually to feel the love of God. Nor is there any true affirming of the resurrection without such honesty.

Jesus himself was so honest that he never gave more answers than there are to be given; and he always gave answer to the questioner more than he did to the question. That integrity accounts for his reply to the Saduccees who sought to make his belief in the resurrection look ridiculous.

They had posed the hypothetical and absurd dilemma to him, asking whose wife a woman would be in the day of resurrection, if she had been married seven times in this life. To this Jesus immediately shows that eternal life is not a mere extension but a transformation of life, that there is neither marriage nor being given in marriage. What matters is not quantity of time but quality of spirit.

Jesus' saying ends all fruitless speculation about the life after. Even to compare that condition with supposedly sexless angels is to declare that there is no way we can even begin to imagine with our minds in time and space what is to come after time and beyond space. The power of God to be eternally with us is affirmed, as in the Lord's proclaiming to Moses in a later generation, "I am (present tense) the God of Abraham...Isaac...and Jacob." Other than that Jesus says nothing more about the afterlife.

Moreover, with the Sadducees as with us, Jesus goes beyond the question to the questioner. He is raising the issue with you and me whether we really know the power of God, the God of the living, not of the dead.

It's at this point that we come to the question whether a seemingly insignificant carpenter, in a backwater country, two millennia ago can still stir faith, hope, and love within us. The ultimate proof of any life beyond the outward burial is what is happening this side of the grave within you and me, and between us in the Spirit of the living Christ.

That is the truth waiting to be validated and which was anticipated when Joseph returned to a newness of life after the "days of weeping" were over. May we live in such gratitude to God who gives us the victory through our Lord Jesus Christ, to whom be the honor, glory, dominion and power, now and forever. Amen.

Humor

The Practice

It was while serving as pastor in a small Oklahoma town thirty years ago that I drove up to my favorite gas station. When the owner came out to service my car (long before the days of self-serve), he said, "Rich, I must admit I've never seen a sermon title like you have for this Sunday." When I asked how that was so, he explained that when passing by the outside bulletin board at the church, he read it as saying, "The Great Comedian!"

Then I realized how a quick glance, at a distance could have given that impression. The actual title was "The Great Come Down!" Displayed as it was in that week before Christmas, the title was an anticipation of a sermon on the Incarnation, as God's coming down to earth in Christ.

But upon second thought, "The Great Comedian" could have served the purpose just as well. For the Incarnation certainly represented heavenly joy transforming our earthly gloom.

Moreover, that incident has set me to thinking over three decades of subsequent ministry how intrinsic is humor to creative ministry. It's not just a matter of injecting that element periodically into sermons, although that is important to the process. Rather humor is one of those necessary dimensions to the whole of leading in worship, education, caring, and even in administrative tasks. Just how "saving humor" functions in the various aspects of congregational life will be suggested in the following reflections.

Worship

Robert Keck in his *Spirit of Synergy* wrote about how meditative prayer has worked for him. He was struck by how when opening himself to God, in a listening rather than in a speaking mode, he would find himself laughing. Suddenly he was led to perceive his life in true perspective, which inevitably included recognizing how ridiculous so much of it must have seemed to "the eye of God."

Certainly in our public as well as private devotions we have endless occasions to give expression to what is declared in Psalm 2, "He who sits in the heavens laughs..." That insight appropriately finds its way into the preaching, for theological and not simply for rhetorical purposes.

Of course, because humor is power, it must be used carefully. The congregation is not well served by clergy who mistake themselves for stand-up comedians. There is a *gravitas* which befits the ministerial calling, which means that clergy will not "try to be funny" either in or out of the pulpit. People's pain and the agony of the world do not lend themselves to facetious treatment.

Yet, as a Scottish saying has it, "Angels can fly because they take themselves lightly." While respecting the seriousness of the life and death issues which it is the worship leader's privilege to address, pastors ought never to take themselves too seriously and certainly never to treat ecclesiastical pomposity as a sacred cow.

The December/January 1979 issue of *Modern Liturgy* was helpfully devoted to this subject. Among the contributions was "Bringing Biblical Humor to Life in Liturgy" by Doug Adams, who has been a leader in the field while teaching at Pacific School of Religion.

Teaching

The model for religious teaching is Jesus, who exemplified for all faith traditions how to puncture the pretenses of hypocrisy. So he was contrasting the legal eagle's trying to pick the speck out of another's eye, while overlooking the 2'x4' in his own eye. So many of Jesus' sayings and parables are replete with ironical twists. Elton Trueblood's *Humor of Christ* was a pioneer work in helping the contemporary generation awaken to how rich and varied was the levity of the Lord. More recently Conrad Hyers has written *And God Created Laughter: The Bible as Divine Comedy.* William H. Willimon's *And the Laugh Shall Be First* is a good treasury of religious humor.

Yet the use of irony by Jesus was always saving in purpose. That emphasis was noted by theologian Reinhold Neibuhr, who reminded us that humor could be used to cut others down, to demean or ridicule them. In contrast Jesus used his wit to wake people up and open them up to the grace of God.

Certainly it has been my experience as a pastor that the way to help people relax, be themselves, and be receptive to whatever it is that is to be communicated is by means of the light touch. Those of us who have long been used to doing things so "decently and in order" need to be increasingly able to give and receive the gift of spontaneity which is inseparable from humor.

In fellowship gatherings it has been my pleasure to share original lyrics set to familiar tunes, with apologies each time to Mark Russell, the musical satirist of note. When the Presbyterian Church was taking its lumps over a much-publicized sexuality report and over other controversial issues, I penned "The Presbyterian Blues," to the tune of "St Louis Blues":

I don't know why I've got those Presbyterian blues.
But if I have 'em, you must have 'em too.
But compared to Jim and Tami,
None of us is in a stew!

An Example

Another experience that well illustrated how humor may help create community was provided in a recent officers' retreat. Such official gatherings are often rather ponderous in tone. But not so in this particular gathering which was led by two lively counselors who combined their talents to lead in a workshop which inspired much laughter and learning. They applied Virginia Satir's *People-Making* categories to the various aspects of the church's life.

So across the top of a long chalk board they listed such elements as "Physical," "Intellectual," "Emotional," "Sensual," "Spiritual," "Interactional," "Nutritional," and "Contextual." Then in the side columns they listed a variety of activities in the church to show how the various aspects of personal life are incorporated into the communal life.

For instance, singing as an activity clearly has significance for emotional and spiritual as well as physical implications. The building of a playscape by dozens of church members brought intellectual and contextual as well as interactional elements into play.

But it was the playing with these interactions which made the retreat the most enjoyable ever experienced by the participants. Costumes were brought to dress various church officers in the elements represented. So when the usually dignified chair of the Finance Committee agreed to put on a "hot-pink" boa to illustrate sensuality, he brought the house down!

Is it stretching the truth to say that the "people who play together pray together"? Certainly it's not too much to expect the infectious humor of the Lord to lighten up our lives in more ways than one.

The Preaching

THE BIRTH OF MIRTH

Genesis 18:1-3,9-14;21:1-7

If as the saying goes, "Laughter is the best medicine", we just got a healthy dose of it. For there is laughter throughout our scripture today.

Sarah got both the first and the last laugh, as she eavesdropped on the conversation with the Lord. When hearing the Almighty declare that a child would be born to her, a ninety year old, and to her husband, Abraham, a hundred year old, she apparently let out enough of a chortle that she got caught in her incredulity.

Although she got scolded for disbelieving that the seemingly impossible could happen, the Lord wasn't too hard on her. For, after all, she really couldn't be blamed for thinking that her leg was being pulled, at the thought that a baby could be born to a childless couple of such advanced years.

Moreover, none of her understandable skepticism prevented the pregnancy from occurring. And once the child came into the world, another occasion for humor presented itself. This came in the form of Abraham's naming of the child.

Now put yourself in his position. What would you have called the newborn? You could have followed the custom of naming him after yourself—in this case, Abraham Jr. But not only would that have been the easy way out, but it would not have fit the rather extraordinary circumstances of the birth. Somehow, God had to figure into the child's name, since the natal surprise was clearly as much the Lord's doing as the human father's.

So, they named the child Isaac. And what does that mean, literally? In the Hebrew, it translates "He (that is, God) laughs." Laughter, then gives definition to Isaac's name, and does, in fact, express a necessity of life.

A Necessity

For, if we take Isaac's coming into the world as the birth of mirth, we will recognize how from life's beginning children bring an innate sense of joy into the world. There's nothing which can light-up a grown-up's face so spontaneously as the sight of a little one. Childhood is meant to be the time when the funny bone is tickled. It was, after all, a young one who identified the emperor as having no clothes on. So Art Linkletter, in his book, *Old Age is Not for Sissies*, says:

> I learned a long time ago that the most interesting interviews are with children or with people older than eighty. Both are refreshingly frank, unaffected by what other people think. Children are too young to know any better. People over eighty...have no time for hypocrisy.

Barriers

But we all know that there is nothing inevitable about a sense of humor. We come into this world with that capability. Yet there are many barriers to keep us from developing it.

At one end of life's spectrum, there is the pressure to grow up too fast. It seems that youngsters are scarcely out of the cradle before some parents are sending them off to computer camp. It looks as if we are doing a replay of The Little Lord Fauntleroy era, when even the clothes were supposed to make little men and women out of children.

Besides that, in the age of television there is too much exposure to too much too soon. That unending flow of bad news over the media is what can take the joy our of life for people of all ages. Joan Collins, the folk singer, confessed that she just had to quit watching or listening to daily broadcasts of current events because they depressed her.

Sometimes you hear people in their later years saying that it gets harder to take things lightly when the world's problems weigh so heavily. Even in a less threatening period in history the temptation was great for people to let life's difficulties get the best of them.

Certainly one of the sadder chapters in the American past was when our foremost humorist lost touch with his gift near life's end. Mark Twain had been making the whole world laugh for most of his days. But then a series of wretched investments put him into financial straits and soured his disposition. Finally, the pre-mature death of a dearly beloved daughter resulted in his letting a dark cloud hang over him continuously.

In contrast, another Abraham—Lincoln—resisted the criticism of clergy who faulted him for his joking in the midst of the Civil War. He told these sanctimonious visitors to the White House, "Unless I could find some surcease from sorrow, my heart would break!"

So the ongoing challenge for us of any age is to keep the bounce in every ounce of our life. The Lord, in the Fourth Gospel, is realistic enough to speak of the necessity of being born again, or born from above—or, to paraphrase, undergo a repeated re-birth of mirth. Baptism in his Spirit means that we are immersed in the everlasting joy of the Lord, which is the ultimate and ongoing source of an up-beat life.

Source

For the divine comedy has been implicit in relationship to the Creator from the beginning. To be made in the image of God is another way of saying that we share in the Maker's sense of humor.

Even the Greeks had a feeling for this when they classified human beings as "laughing animals." Hyenas are said to laugh; but it only seems so. Their young may chase their tails with a sense of play. But only people play with life itself and have the capacity to stand back and gain perspective on the whole.

Only people can grow old gracefully, that is, with an ever expanding sense of life's incongruities. Hyenas and all other creatures become predictably serious as they age. But as George Burns proves, life begins at twice 40.

That's about the time he started playing the role of God in the movies. And it may be that he comes as close to being type-cast as anyone for the part, because he was born Nathan Birnbaum.

Now you don't have to be Jewish to be funny, but it helps. For they are the folks who from the beginning had a sense of the absurd, as summarized in the short couplet,

How odd of God
To choose the Jews.

Even the Jews knew that they didn't deserve the honor and quite often would have been been glad to have been spared the special treatment. For in every subsequent age, they suffered from having been the non-conformists. When undergoing repression and persecution, as has been the Hebrew lot, then one laughs to live, as a matter of survival. That's why it is no accident that Jews have become leading humorists over the centuries.

Perhaps you will recall the rabbi, in *Fiddler on the Roof.* Life in Russia for his people was then proving to be so precarious that he chanted:

May the Lord bless and keep the Czar...
Far away from us!

So has it been for all who have had to make the best of a seemingly impossible situation. That is why I believe it most fitting that the Jewish people descended from Sarah, who despite her age and barren condition could still laugh—even if it appeared sacreligious at the time. She was also the one, who could have the last laugh in the story, because in her gratitude she declared, "God has made laughter for me."

The Question

So we come now to the question for you and me—is God making laughter for us? Do we acknowledge the Lord to be the source of everlasting mirth? Do we show forth that joy as the fruit of the Spirit, not only with our lips but in our lives?

Among those who so evidenced it were those in the early Greek Orthodox Church who on the day after Easter would gather in the sanctuary to tell humorous stories and anecdotes, as the most fitting way to celebrate the big joke that God had pulled on Satan in the resurrection. What could be more appropriate for celebrating the presence of the Risen Lord than with a gaiety reflecting renewed faith through God's power and victory over apparently impossible odds?

It's not that the good cheer is a cover for the pain of grief. It's not that we are called upon to "put on a happy face" in all our relationships. There is, as Ecclesiastes reminds us, "a time to weep and a time to laugh."

There is even a time to hate as well as to love. For in the midst of domestic tranquility, there are conflict and anger. In fact, both exist at the same time, as was well reported by the noted clergy-writer Charlie Shedd. After a set-to with his wife, he found this note on his kitchen counter:

Dear Charlie:
I hate you.
Love, Martha.

Again, I ask of you and me—are we manifesting the renewal of Christ's eternal life within and between us, by letting "the incredible lightness of being" in the love of the Lord overcome the weight of hostility? Are we letting the uplifting power of the Risen Lord help us overcome the daily temptation of becoming "sad sacks"?

May it be, then, that in the Risen Lord we are Isaac to our parents, or to those who are like mothers and fathers to us—so that through us they are able to say "He (God) laughs." May it be that we are like Sarah to our children, or to those who are like sons and daughters to us, so that they too might know "God has made laughter for me..." In so doing may we all be bearing joy as the fruit of the Spirit for one another.

Local History

The Practice

Thomas "Tip" O Neil, former Speaker of the House and U.S. Representative from Massachusetts, was known for his famous aphorism, "All politics is local." There is no question but that all elected officials ultimately derive their power from "the grass roots."

In a comparable way, "All ministry is local." Within that setting, the telling of a locality's story plays a special role.

Recounting the past of a given era may not seem, at first blush, to be a constitutive element of ministry. While religious history courses have long been a part of seminary curriculum, the practice of writing or otherwise highlighting local history has not usually been included in that teaching.

Yet I present the following account as one pastor's vouching for the value of "doing" local history. Before concluding I hope that the reader will have perceived how this aspect of ministry is inseparable from meeting institutional and personal needs within a congregation.

The Precipitating Event

It was in mid-morning on a fall day in 1969 that I looked up from my desk in a Chicago suburban church. On that five-acre site, just outside the office window, I saw two men walking the grounds. Upon inquiring, I learned that they were latter-day relatives of the original pioneers who had farmed that acreage from the 1840s. Back for a family funeral, they were using the occasion to recall early years on the homestead.

That initial incident triggered what has become a two decade-long process. For after arriving at the church five years earlier, I had learned what lack of cohesion there was in that rapidly developing suburb. Situated as it was in betwixt and between six established municipalities, this "instant community" lacked a center. With a 27% annual turnover, I came to call the area "Revolving-Door, Illinois."

Because of that sociological/spiritual vacuum, I began to contact the few residents remaining in the locale from pre-bulldozer days. I visited the county historical society to familiarize myself with the materials on the subject. The intent of the effort was to disseminate information within the congregation about the background of the area into which the members had moved. Soon, however, the story was being shared with a larger audience.

Adjacent to the church a community college was built in the early 1970s. The College of DuPage served the whole of the county, located immediately to the west of Cook County. I inquired whether a course would be offered on the history of the county itself.

When learning that such a study was not planned, I volunteered to develop it. By the spring of 1975, the subject was included in curriculum and continued to be to offered after I moved from the area.

In 1976 I was invited to join a commission to prepare the county's celebration of the nation's bicentennial. Out of that came an anthology, to which I contributed a chapter, my first historical writing.

The Initial Writing

Two books were forthcoming following this initial experience. A layman suggested as part of the congregation's 20th anniversary celebration in 1981 that I write a history of the immediate area. It happened that the natural focal point of the vicinity was The Morton Arboretum. This 1500-acre site had been given by the salt company's founder, Joy Morton, to a foundation in the 1920s. But the story of the institution had not been chronicled previously.

Thus was produced *Around the Arboretum*, an account both of the world's leading "outdoor museum of woody plants" and its neighbors. While the original inspiration for the project came from the church, the publisher was the DuPage Historical Society. The base was thus broadened beyond parochial sponsorship.

The response to this book about the central part of the county led to interest by the Society in underwriting a project which would cover the whole of DuPage. A three-year effort ensued in which I recruited a team of authors who did write-ups on the individual villages and municipalities, while I concentrated on the overall story in the opening six chapters—from the Ice Age to the Fermi National Accelerator, poised as it is on the 21st Century.

DuPage Roots, as I came to entitle it, was published in 1985. It represented the first systematic treatment of the subject since the Federal Writers Project fifty years before. This literary undertaking was the final historical contribution I made to that area before moving to another community.

Transplanted Roots

As it happened, I arrived in Austin, Texas to commence a new pastorate three years before historic Central Presbyterian Church was ready to join in celebrating the city's sesquicentennial. I found myself, therefore, in a position to transplant the historical interest and experience into a new context.

An updated account of the congregation's past was an obvious starting point—the last history having been written fifty years before. A retired journalist and life-long member of the church was the logical choice for authoring the book, with my role becoming a supportive one.

Another member who represents the third generation in the church had long advocated obtaining a state historical commission marker for the site. My arrival proved to be the catalyst by which this objective was accomplished.

Again, I sought to broaden the process beyond the confines of the church itself by agreeing to serve as chair of our presbytery's Bicentennial Committee. It happened, too, that the Presbyterian Church (U.S.A.) was celebrating its 200th birthday at the very same time that the local sesquicentennial was occurring. I had a hand in planning events by which these anniversaries were observed concurrently.

On the Synod level I served on the board of the Presbyterian Historical Society of the Southwest. In that capacity, I led in coordinating an effort for a joint session between the PHSS and the Texas Historical Association.

Preaching has come into play as a means of exercising the ministry of local history. But before describing that worship component, I would place it in the the context of the value of the practice.

Uses of the Past

Herbert J. Muller's *The Uses of the Past* points up the value of the study of history in broad strokes. David E. Kyvig and Myron A. Marty's *Nearby History* provides the rationale for developing local interpretations as well as for delineating a methodology. I propose to add to their insights only by suggesting what has proved worthwhile about the results of historicizing in a parish setting.

Toward that end, I would share a technique used whenever I have had occasion to teach local history. Never assuming that students automatically have any idea as to why any historical study is being pursued, I have offered to "map-out" reasons in terms of a set of first-letter abbreviations—MAP.

"M" represents "motivation," insofar as the study of the past inspires future action. Any looking-back is always toward the possibility of moving ahead.

"A" represents "appreciation." There is intrinsic interest on the part of any individual in where he or she comes from. Corporately, the same is true, as it is better to know than not to know. The "Art for Art's sake" is a principle which applies equally to a recovery of the past.

"P" represents "perspective." Inevitably arising from this recovery is a point of view which is not otherwise evident and which provides direction for forward movement.

Institutionally, the primary benefit of reflecting upon heritage is positive re-enforcement of a congregation's self-identity. To practice good history means reporting "warts and all." But future definition of purpose depends upon drawing upon that which has gone before. I have found this factor to be at work both in a suburban church in the early stages of identifying itself as well as in an established downtown church which has to be re-identifying itself in response to urban challenge.

Nor ought the impact on individuals to be minimized. For the story-telling process as a whole encourages persons to become autobiographical in a healing way. Preaching may also include extended illustrations which arise out of the corporate life of the congregation. At Central Presbyterian Church I converted a critical incident from the past into the following dramatized sermon.

May both the foregoing reflection on one pastor's use of the past and this illustrative homily become a catalyst for others who would use local history as a means for generating creative motivation, appreciation and perspective.

The Preaching

WILL TO LIVE

Joshua 24:1-18

Preacher: What you have just heard is the first in a series of historical reviews. In the Bible such summaries of days-gone-by recur periodically. In addition to this initial retrospective in Joshua, there is the replay of the past found in Ezra, as subsequent events were brought forward to that post-exilic time. In the New Testament Stephen bore comparable witness, including in his summary the life of Jesus, for whose sake he was to be martyred.

But the pattern of events was originally set forth by Joshua. He also modeled the use to which the past was being put in terms of present choices. For it was the term "choose" which he chose to use as the heart of his reflections on the God of Abraham, Isaac, Jacob, and Joseph. Moses declared explicitly in Deuteronomy, "Choose life." Not to keep the moral law, as summarized in the Ten Commandments, would be the equivalent of committing corporate suicide. Joshua's generation, having crossed over into the Promised Land, was confronted by the same critical decision of faithfulness.

Today, of course, we are discerning how that "choice goes by forever," as James Russell Lowell so well expressed the issue in recent times. Whether on a global scale, in regard to the planet's survival, or on the local scene, it continues to be decision-making time in regard to our having a future.

How life is chosen over death in the days to come is suggested by the choice made in the experience of one individual who lived in this community one hundred years ago. He was, in fact, part of this congregation at the time. While later to be identified world-wide as O. Henry, he was in this locality known as William Sidney Porter—or as "Will" to his friends. It is his "will-to-live" which will serve to throw light on the scripture's injunction to faithfulness.

For on April 25, 1898, Porter arrived in Columbus, Ohio, to begin a three-year sentence in the federal penitentiary. He had been convicted of embezzlement. Jenny Lind Porter, in her biography, *Time to Write,* notes how he then showed the defeat and strain of the past two years. Death had claimed his young wife, Athol, seven months before the trial, as it had their infant son before. He had lost his home, his job, and his reputation. A month after his incarceration, he wrote to Athol's mother, Mrs. Roach, in Austin:

Will: (walking down the aisle) "I have tried to reconcile myself to remaining here for a time, but I am about at the end of my endurance. There is absolutely not one thing in life at present or in prospect that makes it of value...I know all the arguments that could be advanced as to why I should endure it, but I have reached the limit of endurance...It would be better for every one else and a thousand times better for me to end the trouble instead of dragging it out."

Preacher: Perhaps just writing that letter helped you in making the decision not to act on your despondency.

Will: Writing had always been important to me; but it became far more so in my imprisonment than in any previous time. If it had not happened in that way, I could easily have used my position as prison pharmacist to end the ordeal.

Preacher: But working those late evening hours, I understand that you did have time to write in a way which you had not before.

Will: It is true that there was much moving about in my earlier years, as I left my birth-state of North Carolina at age nineteen to come to the healthier climate of a Texas ranch and subsequently to Austin where I entered a "whirl-a-gig" of social activity.

Preacher: What was Austin like then?

Will: A friend of mine described it as a merry place in the 1880's. He wrote that "The old burg was filled with cowmen, flush of money, roaring to spend it on gambling, booze and women of the night." He also recalled how I and my friends had good credit at the bar of Doc Muntick who, he said, "could look you in the eye and prescribe a pick-you-up that would put backbone on a rope."

Preacher: How long were you in Austin?

Will: I was here for twelve years, during which time I worked as pharmacist, before trying my hand at a cigar store, then becoming a bookkeeper, after that working as a draftsman for the State Land Office, before ending my career in this town as an ill-fated teller at First National Bank.

Preacher: But between your work and your play, did you not have any time to write while in Austin?

Will: Yes, I submitted contributions to newspapers, and even bought a satirical weekly, Th*e Rolling Stone*, for which I wrote and illustrated. But the Germans in town were especially unhappy with my lampoons, and that light-hearted journal did not endure, so that my early literary efforts proved ephemeral.

Preacher: I must admit surprise in learning how you not only showed talent at writing but for music as well.

Will: I did enjoy it, from choreographing at the Millett Opera House to singing to my daughter Margaret.

Preacher: We've learned in this congregation that you did some singing as a light bass in our choir, along with Mrs Roach and her daughter Athol, your wife-to-be.

Will: Yes, and it was the pastor of the church, Richmond Kelley Smoot, who led us in our wedding vows. On July 1, 1887, we obtained our wedding license, hired a city carriage, and made our way to his home for the service. His twelve-year-old son, Lawrence, was a witness.

Preacher: You will be pleased to know that the home in which the two of you lived has been preserved and is open for later generations to visit.

Will: Any who go into that dwelling should remember that the muslin curtains and wicker chair were bought with the money I had saved for Athol to go to the Chicago World's Fair. But she spent it on our home, and for me, instead. It was that sacrifice which prompted me later to write "The Gift of the Magi."

Preacher: Your faith clearly meant more to you than just making literary references to the Bible.

Will: How much it meant to both of us was evidenced after she contracted tuberculosis and so was not able to sing. Thus on a Sunday morning, I would take her in the carriage to the west side of the church, where the windows were open and we could hear the choir together.

Preacher: Her death must have grieved you deeply.

Will: It wasn't that I just missed having her with me. Her faithfulness had always given me hope for the future. After the charges of embezzlement had been dropped initially, it was Athol who encouraged me to take the position as a columnist when the opportunity was offered by the *Houston Post*.

And while she believed in me as a writer with capabilities beyond newspapers, she knew I had to leave Austin. Although not physically well enough to make the move, she and six-year-old Margaret joined me.

Preacher: But when the charges were revived, you fled the country.

Will: Shamefully, I must admit to that. Yet when news of Athol's imminent death reached me in Honduras, I knew that I had to be faithful to the one who had been so to me. I came back to Austin to be with her and to accept the arrest. She never withdrew her support of me, despite my weakness for drink. So I entered the penitentiary in despair.

Preacher: But you left that imprisonment having written the first of the stories which were to become renowned the world over. You gave the ultimate surprise ending during those last nine years in New York City, when you were writing as many as one story a week. How could you have risen above the temptation to self-pity, self-condemnation, self-destruction to have given the world such an unforgettable legacy?

Will: Perhaps I would best let one of my own stories provide the answer. Just remember that I put myself in them, particularly this one, which I called *The Last Leaf*, a title suggested by an Oliver Wendell Holmes poem. In the story I have the narrator say:

Narrator: (as actors appear) It was to quaint old Greenwich Village that the art people came hunting for north windows and low rents. At the top of a three-story brick, Sue and Johnsy had their studio. One from Maine and the other from California, they had met at a restaurant on 8th Street and had found their tastes so congenial that they jointly rented a studio.

That was in May. In November, a cold, unseen stranger, called Pneumonia, stalked the colony, touching one here and there with his icy fingers. Johnsy , whose blood had been thinned by California zephyrs, was smitten. She lay, scarcely moving from her iron bedstead. She had strength only to gaze through the panes of the apartment's Dutch window, across at the backside of the brick building on the other side of the street.

A doctor was called in for treatment. After several visits, the physician one morning invited Sue into the hallway, saying:

Doctor: She has one chance in ten—and that chance is for her to want to live. Your little lady made up her mind that she's not going to get well. I will do all that science can accomplish. But whenever my patient begins to count the carriages in her funeral procession, I subtract 50% from my curative remedies.

Narrator: After the doctor had gone, Sue returned to Johnsy 's room with a drawing board, thinking Johnsy asleep. As she was quietly sketching, she was startled as she turned to find her roommate with eyes open wide, looking out the window and counting the leaves falling from an old gnarled ivy vine on the building opposite.

Johnsy : Six. They're falling faster now. Three days ago, there were almost a hundred. When the last one falls, I must go too. I've known that for three days.

Sue: Oh, I've never heard of such nonsense. What have old ivy leaves to do with your getting well? Johnsy dear, promise me to keep your eyes closed and not look out the window until I am done working. Try to sleep. I must call Behrman up to be my model for the old hermit picture.

Narrator: Old Behrman was a painter who lived on the ground floor beneath them. He was past sixty and had always been about to paint a masterpiece; but he had never begun it, instead smelling strongly of juniper berry. He earned a little by serving as model to those young artists in the Village who could not pay the price of a professional.

Sue told him of Johnsy 's fancy, how she would, light and fragile as a leaf herself, float away when her slight hold on the world grew weaker.

They went upstairs while Johnsy was still sleeping. They peered fearfully out the window at the vine. A persistent cold rain, mixed with snow, was falling. Sue then pulled the shade down to the window sill as Old Beherman made his way back below.

When Sue awoke the next morning, she found Johnsy with dull, wide-open eyes staring straight at the drawn green shade.

Johnsy : Pull it up! I want to see.

Narrator: Wearily, Sue obeyed. And, lo, after the beating rain and fierce gusts of wind, there yet stood out against the brick wall, one ivy leaf—the last on the vine. Still dark green near its stem, but with edges tinged with yellow, it hung bravely from a branch twenty feet above the ground.

Johnsy : I've been a bad girl, Susie. Something has made the last leaf stay there to show me how willful I was. It's wrong to want to die. Bring me a little broth now. I need to get back to my painting.

Narrator: The doctor came that afternoon and afterward reported to Sue that her roommate would live. But it was not to be with the old man downstairs, Behrman. The janitor had found him that morning, icy cold, his clothing and shoes wet through. No one could imagine where he been on such a dreadful night. But a lantern was discovered across the street and a ladder, and a pallet with green and yellow colors mixed on it.

Preacher: Yes, Behrman had painted his masterpiece on the wall, by the vine, on the night that the last leaf fell. This truth-in-fiction found its counterpart in the life of William Sidney Porter himself, redeemed as he was by sacrificial love. Are we not also inspired to "choose life" because of Will's will to live? May those who are to come after in this church look back upon our generation and say of us, in the words of Emily Dickinson:

> A death blow is a life blow to some,
> Who till they died, did not alive become.

Media Ministry

The Practice

Among the items I unpacked upon moving to Austin, Texas, in mid-1986 was a set of video-tapes. This collection contained copies of programs in which I had participated as host for The Church Federation of Greater Chicago over the preceding three years. Most of these programs had been broadcast on the ABC affiliate in Chicago.

Upon arriving in the capital city of Texas, I learned that there had not been a history of ecumenically-sponsored public service broadcasts. My past experience led me to begin an exploration of such a possibility in my new hometown.

The Preparation

I soon identified two immediate sources of support for the concept. One was a member of my congregation, an Assistant Professor of Journalism at the University of Texas who taught in the broadcast sequence in the College of Communication. Because he was willing to serve as producer of a series, he brought a technical expertise which added weight to a proposal.

Also essential to the process was the willingness of the Austin Area Conference of Churches (AACC) to be the sponsor of the program in cooperation with whatever station might agree to provide time, a studio, and staff for directing and taping. An ecumenical/inter-faith sponsorship assured non-sectarian programming. It was the local CBS affiliate which responded favorably with an offer of a thirteen week series to be aired early on Sunday mornings starting in March, 1988.

The immediate need was to bring a team together, including others to share in the hosting and program development. Because I was new to the Austin scene, it was necessary to find colleagues who knew both the larger and religious communities. Among those who have shared in the hosting are the Bishop of the Austin Diocese of the Catholic Church, a Lutheran pastor, a young woman student from the Hillel Foundation with broadcast experience, and an African American Methodist woman pastor.

The purpose of the public service broadcast, entitled *Austin Faith Dialogue*, was defined as highlighting the interaction of the religious community and the greater Austin area. The programs were to be public affairs discussions and presentations, as distinct from worship services or any attempts to proselytize. The emphasis was to be on local rather than global issues. Decisions about content and participants were to be determined by a broadcast commission. The tapes were to remain the property of AACC and the station gave permission for them to be replayed on public-access channels.

Preparation included "practice" time before a camera. The church served by the Lutheran pastor had purchased video-equipment, which was made available for the hosts to develop interview skills, with the help of the station news anchor.

The History

It seemed fitting that the first program should feature the ecumenical life of Austin. After four and a half decades of service in the city, the AACC received a sustained recognition in the initial half-hour broadcast. The Austin History Center provided pictures of religious life of the capital of the Texas Republic soon after its 1839 founding, thereby placing the subject in a broader context.

Continuing efforts were made to vary the "talking heads" format. The station made film clips available from its file when the topics of hunger and affordable housing were treated. When the Curator of the Harry Ransom Center at the University of Texas was interviewed about its Gutenberg Bible, he brought prints of the events surrounding the procurement of this cultural/religious icon. On that same program, entitled "The Letter and Spirit of the Word," two high school thespians enacted a scene from *Inherit the Wind*, which sharpened the issue of biblical significance in the larger society.

Variety of subjects and their treatment has proved to be an on-going criterion. Austin happens to be the center of three theological seminaries, each of which were represented in one program, "The Making of Ministers." On the Sunday before Passover, that observance was interpreted by a rabbi and a family from his congregation. Easter practices were compared from Catholic, Orthodox and Protestant perspectives the following week.

The station was pleased with the quality of the initial effort. So the offer was made to continue the production for a full year. That responsiveness was another expression of a cooperation which has been generously extended into its eighth year, even though the station has since changed ownership and management. The Nielsen ratings have shown that program has been tuned in by some five thousand households, although continuation of the series has never been dependent upon the number of viewers.

In the intervening years I have been privileged to interview a variety of leaders from across the nation and world who have found their way to Austin. These have included Bill Moyers who brought his newly-produced *Amazing Grace* PBS special for premiering in the city. The newly named national director of SANE/FREEZE, the Rev. William Sloane Coffin Jr., was on hand for the program when he was helping organize the local chapter. Sarah Weddington, the winning attorney in the Roe vs. Wade case, spoke on how growing up as a Methodist minister's daughter gave shape to her public service career.

The key factor in continuing the series remains the team of hosts and producers, who have changed several times over. A two hour planning session every quarter, with a subsequent division of labor, has meant that each participant has averaged no more than three hours for each week that he or she is involved in the half–hour broadcast.

AACC has long since veen replaced by Austin Metropolitan Ministries. So our programming has reflected the diverse constituency of the religious community, highlighting such faith traditions as Hindus, Muslims, and Sikhs, as well as those of the Christian and Jewish communities. With the Branch Davidian Compound crisis having erupted just an hour's drive north of Austin, we had occasion to do a special program on cults.

The program possibilities have always exceeded the time alloted by the station. But whatever happens in the future, the significance of this undertaking has become clear.

The Significance

Our local media-experiment serves as an example of what William F. Fore describes in his definitive book on the subject, *Television and Religion—The Shaping of Faith, Values, and Culture:*

> The objective here is to develop programs on TV which, within the very midst of TV's expressions of secular worldview and power, nevertheless attempt to illuminate the human condition, to ask meaningful religious questions, to rediscover religious truths, and to find new religious vocabulary which can have meaning for multitudes of men and women today...a number of local councils of churches and other broad–based religious groups have managed to get a significant airing of news from a religious perspective on their local stations. The objective is not to present *the* religious view on any subject. Rather, the aim is to generate robust discussion and debate about the significant issues of the day from many different religious perspectives and viewpoints.

To facilitate the achievement of that purpose, it is desirable for a commercial station to make time and facilities available for programming. The possibilities for reaching a wider public are thereby augmented.

Public-access programs, as Fore describes them, are "narrowcasting." Cable plays a unique role through the requirements to include locally-produced programming, with the religious community allowed equal access. Yet the segmented audience limits the outreach. The best combination has been made possible in Austin, where the commercial station has permitted the program to be replayed at a later time on access channels.

The extent of cooperation between the station and the religious community suggests the multi-faceted value of this ministry. The "networking" has served to develop a positive spirit within and among the participating congregations and religious agencies.

I have interpreted the meaning of this experience to my congregation as a form of outreach, a testimony of how a church's commitment extends beyond parochial concerns. Moreover, I cannot help but have a sense of Providence at how the various elements fell into place at the beginning and how well the series has continued to prosper over a seven year period.

While no two communities are alike, so that the way things work in one place does not necessarily mean that they will in another, the principles implicit in the above description are likely to be similar. It is certainly encouraging in an era of deregulation to report an instance of media people prepared to swim against the prevailing current by extending rather than contracting public service time.

Other Outlets

The stimulus of doing such public affairs programming has led to other outlets in exercising media ministry. In the 1990s video-conferencing has become a broadening avenue of communication within the religious community, as well as in industry. The airlines have been complaining that business has fallen off due to the Fortune 500 companies' increased use of video-conferencing. Likewise has it become evident to denominational structures and seminaries that it becomes more cost effective to conduct meetings and classes through what has been generically been called "distance learning."

My particular experience at organizing and hosting local television programs has led me into this related field as well. It has been through the Synod of the Sun of the Presbyterian Church USA, the four state area of Texas, Oklahoma, Arkansas, and Louisiana, in cooperation with Austin Presbyterian Theological

Seminary that I have led in developing such educational videoconferences.

One, fittingly, was on the theme of "Developing Christian Community in an Electronic Age." That is a key issue, whether it is possible to develop "I-Thou" relationships using "I-It" media, to use Martin Buber's terminology.

There is no question that a growing number of faith communities have brought that technology into play. The Mormons have for twenty years downlinked broadcasts world–wide in their churches throughout the world which have been uplinked in Salt Lake City, thus tying that communion closer together. Likewise the Pentecostal, Catholic, Episcopal and Methodist communities have made ever more frequent use of it.

Even local congregations have far more access to the rich variety of programs which are transmitted by satellites orbiting 22,000 miles above the earth. Receiving dishes are becoming inexpensive enough to be within range of many congregations.

Certainly every congregation needs to be involved in media literacy for its communicants. I have taught courses in denominational workshops on Television Awareness Training because of my conviction that everyone resides in and is surrounded by that sea of electronic influence. Not to be conscious of that all-pervasive influence is like the proverbial fish which was asked how it liked living in the ocean. To this it replied, "What ocean?"

"The Power of Image" is a curriculum, featuring an excellent video, produced by the Friendship Press in 1990, which best communicates how young people and adults alike can become more pro-active in relationship to media. Producing in-house programs, now that video cameras are so readily available, can become a positive way to make use of the technology.

It is certainly not enough for the mainline churches to rail against the televangelists as selling out the gospel, although that is often the case. Nor is it a sufficient response to take pride in not watching much television, even though so much of it is a wasteland. Rather it is imperative for clergy to assume leadership in interpreting the theological and ethical dimensions of the communications revolution through which we are passing. The following sermon is one example of an effort in that direction.

The Preaching

The Image Makers

Acts 17:16-31

This story invites us to use our imagination, insofar as Paul refers to the human imagination. He speaks of this, fittingly, in Athens where the creation of architects and sculptors had reached its peak.

At first blush, the text seems the opposite of being inviting. For the apostle is sounding an obvious warning by declaring a Jewish message to his Gentile audience. Without quoting the second of the Ten Commandments explicitly, he nevertheless brings that idol-making prohibition to bear in the midst of a Greek setting.

Yet, as a Hellenist, Paul even quotes their own poets to his listeners to prove his point. Drawing from the literary imagination of the Stoic poets, he implicitly expresses appreciation for the artistic impulse within the human soul.

That mixed reaction to our image-making powers continued throughout all subsequent centuries, into our own era. The best treatment of that subject which I have seen comes from the hand of George S. Heyer in his *Signs of the Times.* His book on Christian aesthetics sets forth the continuing tension between letting the *imago dei* within us find fulfillment and guarding against the idolatrous misuse of that divine gift. From the iconoclasts in Byzantium to the builders of Chartres Cathedral, from Savonarola to Rembrandt, that struggle for faithful expression of imagination "goes by forever."

But in our own time, the issue has assumed Titanic proportions. For we live in in era which has reversed the previous aphorisms. Invention has now become the mother of necessity. We have come so to depend upon our gadgets that we cannot imagine ourselves living without them.

TV—The Key

Of all these, none is more determinative than television—the work of image-makers, *par excellence.* Marshall McLuhan, who might rightly be denominated The Prophet of the Electronic Age, observed that TV is not simply one among a number of inventions of the modern age, rather, it is the key one that sets the tone and direction for today's—and tomorrow's—societies.

McLuhan correctly observes that this instantaneous communication is converting the earth into a "global village." Any one of us is apt to know more about trapped whales in the Arctic than about the persons down the street, or even next door. This media is transforming our politics (rendering parties obsolete), our education (expecting to be entertained), our religion (engendering arm-chair faith, via televangelists), and every other institution.

Moreover McLuhan's dictum that "the media is the message" (his original term was the "massage") gives the most complete expression to this revolution of consciousness. Apart from the content of programs, the very act of watching unless consciously offset, will dictate a passive mind-set, a simplistic view of problem solving (half-hour segments), and shortened attention-spans (twin to instant gratification).

Indeed, the former Dean of the Annenberg School of Communication at the University of Pennsylvania notes how much religious significance television has assumed. "Television is an environment. You are born into it. You absorb its effects by the time you can speak. It's like a religion of the pre-industrial age. It tells all the stories, gives a coherent view of how the world works, and what standards of conduct are normal. It's the modern myth-maker, the oracle telling who wins and who loses."

We are now into still another generation of children who spend more time in front of the television set than in school, certainly than in conversation with the family, and most certainly than in the church. Interviews with teens who deny knowing poetry show that they know more than realize. Although not being able to repeat passages of Shakespeare or scripture by heart, they are able to recite by the hour lyrics (likely not recognized as poetry) from the popular songs absorbed from listening to the radio or from watching MTV.

With a set on in a home on the average of six and a half hours a day, it is, therefore, not surprising to learn that children between the ages of five and eighteen years of age will see a thousand commercials a week. Surveys have shown an average of eight violent episodes per hour on any given channel.

Becoming Aware

Of course, as those made in the image of God, with the capacity of reflection and self-awareness, we have a choice as to whether to remain passive or not in the face of this onslaught of images. The Amish show forth a clear alternative by their valiant efforts to be neither "in" nor "of the world." Even short of such rejection of modern technology, we are able to choose whether to use rather than be used by the media.

How close to home this faith may be practiced was discerned in a household where a visiting pastor found a mother and child watching television. The parent turned off the set as the visit began. The child complained about the audio-visual loss. The mother explained that when there was company nothing should come in the way of people paying attention to one another other. By keeping the priorities straight, by putting people first, that parent modeled a countervailing alternative to an all-too-prevalent lifestyle.

As that determination to control rather than be controlled by the works of our hands is expanded, then families may well find themselves declaring television off-limits during meal-time. Deliberate choices are made as to which programs are watched and periodic discussions are incorporated about the viewing, so that little ones begin to develop an early objectivity about the difference between images and reality. Christians do well to beware the slant and bias built into television programming.

We might even come up with our own Decalogue of TV viewing, which would certainly include, "Thou shalt not let the commercials make you covetous." Even jingles to rival those which are absorbed un-awares from the wave-notes about us may be in order. Try, for instance, this lyric of confession and petition devised by a church school class, to the tune of "I Want to Teach the World to Sing" (the melody of which was once used as a Coca Cola advertisement):

> O, how I love to watch TV,
> Yet, have eyes that don't see.
> O, how I want my TV near,
> Yet have ears that don't hear.
>
> Lord, help us to see,
> When we watch TV,
> With our eyes open wide
> That you are our guide.

That process of self-innoculation against the spiritual pollution of modern image-making is by no means limited to people of biblical faith. Paul in his preaching before the altar to the unknown god at the Aereopagus spoke of all persons in every nation having sought God. "In him we live and move and have our being."

Whether identified as the God of Abraham, Isaac, and Jacob, or as the God and Father of our Lord Jesus Christ, or not, the principle of integrity is at work among all persons. The Spirit of the Maker is indeed in, under, around and through all.

Creative Response

But what persons of the Judeo-Christian tradition are in good position to do is to warn against misuse of images—graven or otherwise and to show forth the positive use of that creative impulse. The lyric from the hymn "Eternal God, Whose Power Upholds" gives magnificent expression to that aspiration:

> O God of beauty, oft revealed In dreams of human art,
> In speech that flows to melody, In holiness of heart:
> Teach us to ban all ugliness That blinds our eyes to Thee,
> Till all shall know the loveliness Of lives made fair and
> free.

As you and I provide living examples of the imaginative life wedded to love, we will gain ever greater appreciation of the one who embodied the truth. His consistency has, in this electronic era, moved my Muse to write:

> The medium is the message,
> We've rediscovered now.
> It's not always what is said,
> But the way, the means, the how.
>
> It's not just what TV shows,
> But the instantaneous way it goes.
> Cross earth, cross sea
> In simultaneity.
>
> But this medium is only an echo
> Of one long ago,
> Yet one who comes today
> In an ever miraculous way.
>
> "The Word became flesh"—
> Form and substance mesh.
> Beyond words, the Word
> Makes our prayers heard.
>
> "Practice what you preach"—
> Twixt word and deed no breach.
> We say; don't do.
> He did, helps us more to.

Outreach

The Practice

The motivation for outreach in any Christian congregation arises from the gospel's mandate to share the good news. Certainly the decline of membership over recent decades in mainline churches is a cause for concern.

In Matthew 6:33 Jesus spoke of seeking first the kingdom. So growth for growth's sake is not the objective. Yet there is no inconsistency between that priority and reaching out intentionally.

If is fitting, therefore, to devise an approach which identifies the uniqueness of a particular fellowship, as it reflects the love of Christ. Such a plan may be defined as *AIM to Grow,* in which the "A" means to Attract, the "I" to Invite, the "M" to Minister.

Attract

Attraction means that a given congregation needs to function as a "magnet church." Attractiveness arises from a congregational life which provides a rich quality of spiritual development, including its worship, nurture, and mission. The program should have sufficient distinctiveness to it that the congregation will be filling a particular niche in God's spiritual ecology.

That intrinsic magnetism will be augmented by ways and means of making known a faith community's unique character. Attraction implies a systematic program of publicity, of letting "your light shine." A communications committee is a vehicle by which regular articles can be submitted to local newspapers.

Attract implies being attractive even in regard to the appearance of building and grounds. As with personal appearance, there is a difference between false pride and a legitimate regard to how we present ourselves. While a morally courageous community will take stands which do not pander to the lowest common denominator, there is every reason to be an inviting people.

Invite

Invitation means that each member of the church has an individual role to play. Research shows that eighty five percent of the people visiting a congregation come because they were invited by someone who is already a member of the congregation.

In a society as highly mobile as ours, there is special opportunity to interpret an invitation to take part in a church community as a means of "putting down roots." Like other clergy of this era, I have found myself ministering in the midst of high turn-over areas. This has led me to write another set of lyrics to set forth the necessity of not waiting to become involved in the life of a faith community. Entitled, " Bloom Where You Are Planted," it may be sung to the tune most commonly associated with "The Church's One Foundation."

O bloom where you are planted,
Take root where'er you live.
To you the Lord has granted
The power to love and give.
Though oft we come and go,
Whate'er the length of stay,
The time is ripe to grow
In the Church's nurturing way.

We've come from wide and far
Like seeds from many a clime,
Whate'er our talents are
To serve this place and time.
Sustained by faith's rich earth,

Flower forth in deeds of love.
Upheld by hope and mirth,
We praise the Son above.

We're part of a larger field,
Brought forth by grace's sun.
Our fruits to God we'll yield,
Eternal life begun.
O bloom where you are planted,
Take root where'er you live.
To you the Lord has granted
The power to love and give.

Minister

Ministry means caring for people as they come and become part of the fellowship. A program of following up on visitors needs to be in place, including prompt subsequent personal contact by the pastor and laity. For those who continue to visit, an invitation to attend an inquirer's class is also in order.

I have had occasion to prepare a booklet called "Sense of Belonging," which is used for such orientation. This basic human need to be part of a support group is the starting point. But within the faith community that belonging has special meaning. To be a member as distinct from being a "friend of the church" is similar to the difference between marrying and dating someone. The depth of commitment in terms of attendance, participation and financial support spells the difference.

Assimilation into membership also involves finding a "support group" within the church. This process entails a "growing edge" of communities within the congregation. Existing groups should be willing and able to reach out—from youth fellowships to an older adult ministry. New groups will also evolve in response to particular needs.

Conclusion

AIM takes its inspiration from I Corinthians 14:1—"Make love your aim." For it is the love of Christ which attracts, invites and ministers through each member and through all together.

The Preaching

By Invitation

Acts 8:26-40

The end of this story serves as a good beginning. For the concluding request that the Ethiopian makes, to be baptized, stands in marked contrast to another who was seeking God in Asia. That other had come to a holy man who took him to a river and held his head below the surface so long that the inquirer had to force his way up, gasping for breath. The teacher then said, "When your soul longs for God as much as your body craves air, then you will find what you seek."

That comparison is striking. Despite the similarity of two persons seeking God and the use of water in both stories, the parallel ends there. For the difference between the gospel and the world's religions is that in Christ God is seeking us more than we seek God. It is God who takes the initiative, who issues the invitation.

The Invitation

From beginning to end this particular story, like the gospel as a whole, has to do with inviting and being invited, and with our response to both. Sometimes we must decide to answer last minute invitations, as well as those sent well in advance.

As we focus first on Philip, we find that being found by God often involves "acting on impulse." For the story begins and ends with the evangelist making abrupt, seemingly impetuous changes in direction. At the beginning an angel directs him to go south; so, he's off to a desert road in the middle of nowhere. Once having encountered the eunuch and fulfilled the purpose he had for him, "the Spirit caught up Philip," and without so much as a "tip of his hat," he was off to the northern end of the region.

That leading is like astronomer Alan Sandage who was on his way home from the observatory one night when he suddenly got an inspiration as to where to direct his telescope to find an elusive signal from the heavens. He immediately turned his car around and in playing his hunch found that his intuition was confirmed, as the first observable pulsar came into view.

More down-to-earth, the biblical story is about Philip's reaching out spatially, and the eunuch's reaching out spiritually. Spatially the evangelist is shown to be opening up new territories. For the first time, an emissary of the church had reached as far south as Gaza and as far north as Caesarea.

But also there is the other person reaching out for spiritual guidance. This Ethiopian eunuch is aimless. Yet his seeking and thirsting for understanding makes him particularly appealing to our questing modern generation.

Perhaps we should begin with the fact that the Ethiopian had status, which by all outward appearances made him look like "the man who had everything." He was, after all, a member of the cabinet, treasurer to the queen of Ethiopia, entrusted with all her wealth.

Despite his being so high up in affairs of the world, he had been made a eunuch. Males were not trusted in the courts with queens. So it is no accident that the passage he should have fixed upon was about humiliation—the Old Testament prophecy describing the Servant of the Lord:

> In his humiliation justice was denied him.
> Who can describe his generation?
> For his life is taken from the earth.

His selection of that one text showed how just beneath the surface of his successful life was a sense of shame. Beyond the taking away of his manhood, the eunuch had his hope of posterity stripped from him. Children were, within the traditional view, believed to be the means by which one's influence on earth continued. No wonder he was struggling with how to come to terms with the loss at justice being denied him.

So simply by patting the seat and inviting someone to sit beside him the eunuch was implying a world of significance. He was looking for nothing less than a reason to go on living.

Before continuing with the response to the invitation, let us pause just long enough to appreciate how the eunuch's problem really is our problem. Certainly a primary cause for emotional disorder is loss of self esteem. The human creature can stand anything, it seems, except the loss of face. Yet Christianity is often, if mistakenly, identified with such a self-denying religion that one seeks to be rid of all pride.

False pride, to be sure, is foolish and destructive. But to be embarrassed, to be robbed of self-respect, to be made a fool of is what will cause even people of faith to withdraw. Like the eunuch, we too are looking for a way to live with genuine pride and hope.

The Response

So we too will invite along side us others who are attuned to our need. Instead of engaging in the usual small talk, upon first meeting, Philip asked, "Do you understand what you are reading?" The question shows that the evangelist perceived the source of hurt, "In his humiliation justice was denied him." The question implies that there is an answer.

Thus, for the first time ever, the connection was made between what has been called the Suffering Servant, described in the book of Isaiah, and Jesus. We are able to infer that Philip explained to the Ethiopian that Jesus knew what it was like to be humiliated—that he had, in fact, let himself be led like a lamb to the slaughter, yet in such a way as to save the face of all. Nonetheless, that life had not ended, and was evident in the one who was bringing the good news.

Once the eunuch saw that connection and felt himself at one with him who had transcended humiliation, he quite naturally asked, "What is to prevent my being baptized?" But let us not conclude before we recognize how the Ethiopian's response is in contrast with the attempted conversions by hard-sell evangelists.

I am reminded of spouses who marry in order "to reform" their husbands or wives, while in healthy marriage, partners will help draw out the other's potential. It is a mutual process and it does not suppose any preconceived model. It always begins with an acceptance of another as he or she is, rather than with a crusading spirit of making somebody over.

D.T. Niles, the great witness for Christ in Asia, gave classical expression to the spirit of sharing the good news. Evangelism, he said, is like "One hungry beggar coming to tell another where food is to be found."

So was the Ethiopian ready to show outward identification with the Suffering Servant, whom he knew to be identifying so empathetically with him. Nothing could then prevent his "going on his way rejoicing"—not even the abrupt departure of the one who had brought him together with the Lord.

As we say goodbye to those who have been so nurturing, even to the point of enabling us to go on living, the temptation is to want to keep the relationship immediate and present forever. Yet that's the beauty of holiness. Though spatially apart, we remain spiritually forever present in the Communion of Saints. And the invitation goes by forever, as you and I extend the gracious offer of the Lord to others, thereby making every ending occasion for a new beginning.

Preaching

The Practice

No series on "Preaching the Practice" would be complete without including preaching itself. Among the aspects of parish practice, preaching plays a distinctive role.

Evidence of how special that role is may be found in the work of pastor search committees. Members of these groups travel to hear prospective pastors preach. If distance precludes a visit to a worship service, the tapes of candidates sermons are requested.

Not only does preaching serve as a determinative standard in pastoral selection, but it also remains high in worship priority, especially within the Protestant tradition, Visitors to a Sunday service are likely to decide whether to return or to become members based on what comes from the pulpit. For those who already belong to a congregation, the preaching gives incomparable focus to what is happening within that particular religious community.

Despite the justifiable aversion to "Prince of the Pulpit" melodramatics, or to the Elmer Gantry-like manipulations of televangelists, preaching deserves especially close attention by its practitioners. All dimensions of the homiletical act need to be intentionally developed and re-developed over the life of a pastorate. The preacher is called continually to prepare with the context, content and delivery in mind.

The Context

The context is the most subtle of the dimensions. Yet the setting in which sermon content is developed and delivered is so vital that a sermon about preaching could well be included at the beginning of any pastorate. Those in the pews need to know "where the preacher is coming from" in terms of what would otherwise be unspoken assumptions.

On an on–going basis it is needs of the people, both individually and as a congregation, which serve as the basis for preaching. Relevance is a term which has been taking a "bad rap" recently. But unless a living connection is made upon each occasion of worship, and made rather quickly in the homily, the speaker is apt to lose the listeners.

St. Augustine identified these three principles of preaching: to hold, to instruct, and to persuade. Having first been imbued in the discipline of rhetoric, Augustine brought the best of public speaking to preaching.

But what makes a sermon more than a speech is that holding people's interest is for a greater recreative purpose than mere entertainment. To instruct is toward the end of gaining insight into dealing redemptively with dilemmas. To persuade is to come under the influence of the Holy Spirit in regard to our decisions and actions.

In 1925 Reinhold Neibuhr, as a Detroit preacher, could not ignore the rising power of the Ku Klux Klan in that city. His addressing that disorder served as a turning point in his career. Likewise will any preacher learn to identify those critical incidents where a congregation resides, and give compelling expression to its joys and sorrows.

What and how I preach in my sixties is not the same as how I was preaching in my twenties. Particularly over the last five years, since learning of my wife's cancer, have I been able to preach with deeper feeling about taking nothing for granted, about being grateful for every day. Who the preacher is as a person at any given point of his or her development is fundamental to the context.

That personal component has always been paramount, whether so recognized or not. "What you are speaks so loudly I cannot hear what you say" has long been one way of defining the indispensable nature of this factor. In the modern world, which is undergoing such unprecedented change, the example set by the pastor as a growing person, both in and out of the pulpit, largely establishes the authority of the spoken word. In an increasingly anonymous society, evidence of the pastor's care and compassion gives credence to the message. Faced with so many threats to our corporate future, the pulpiteer must "practice what is preached," in regard to courage, if the exhortation is not to sound empty.

Instrumental in my hearing the call to ministry was a pastor in the church of my childhood. One morning he appeared in the chancel with a face bruised black and blue. The word had already circulated in the town that he had earlier in the weekend been brutalized by an emotionally-distraught parishioner. Just before the sermon, an elder arose to announce that the pastor would not be filing charges against the assailant. The pastor then proceeded to preach on the lectionary text for the day, from that part of The Lord's Prayer which states, "Forgive us our debts, as we forgive our debtors." I shall never forget both that word and deed of forgiveness!

Moreover, this incident represents another element of the context, the biblical environment. Without interpreting and being interpreted by scripture, a sermon certainly devolves into mere speech-making. It is at this point of probing the integrity of interpretation that the transition must be made to the second dimension of preaching.

The Content

Content and context blend inseparably in scripture. Thus it is that the lectionary provides an important starting point in considering what is preached. For its purpose is to insure a comprehensive treatment of scripture and to help the preacher remain true to its central motifs.

The lectionary also contributed to my use of the computer. Its organizational framework provided impetus to devise a system of organizing sermon material. Using a database program I established the following categories, the meaning of which is illustrated by these entries:

Title	Text	Lectionary	Date	File
Beyond Comparison	JN 01:9-34	A EP 02	87/01/18	K1/01
Bloom Where Planted	JER 29:04-13	X XX XX	87/10/25	K2/03
Dying to Live	JN 12:20-33	B LT 05	88/03/20	K2/05

For example, first entry represents lectionary year A, on the second Sunday of Epiphany. The X XX XX represents a text not included in the lectionary cycle. The file information in the third entry includes the cassette tape drawer code K and the number of the diskette upon which the written copy is stored, 05.

Incidentally, the word processor revolutionized my sermon preparation. My initial response to the prospect of composing electronically was negative. Somehow I had myself convinced that the Holy Spirit flowed more readily through pen and ink (beyond the quill and scroll, but short of the ball-point variety). But the liberation which came from not having to worry about making mistakes, which are so easily corrected on a screen, brought an unexpected sense of grace.

Another surprise was that "one thing leads to another." Something about the very process of composing in this almost "stream-of-consciousness" way results in thoughts, images, and memories arising that were not presenting themselves before. The number of written sermons, has, accordingly, multiplied, making them so much more readily distributable to the congregation. The need for eye contact with the congregation and for openness to spontaneous inspiration in any given preaching moment means that the script is not read, but used as guide. Yet the fullness of preparation makes for an overflowing cup.

Another irony, when considering content, is that biblical preaching depends upon non-biblical illustrations and insights. Jesus' copious use of images and parables has been the inspiration for all vibrant preaching in subsequent ages. The creative connection must be made between the eternal Word and the contemporary scene, if the former is not to be thought of as only in the past tense and the latter is to make present/future sense.

As the years have passed I find that pastoral experience increasingly provides the illustrations which give authenticity to scriptural exposition. No confidences need be disclosed, as no real names are used, and the described incidents are far removed space and time. Moreover, there is truth-in-fiction when strands of experience are woven into a whole new scenario.

The issue of the preacher's making personal disclosure is an on-going one. On the one hand, willingness to let the congregation in on his or her pilgrim's process is a necessary means of showing trust and vulnerability. On the other hand, too frequent self-revelation runs the risk of indecent exposure.

At this point, the transition from what is said to the manner of speaking emerges naturally. For both substance and method must arise from the same sincerity if one has made the passage beyond the outward signs of ordination to the inward confirmation of the call.

Delivery

The "Method School" of acting seems to have left its mark on homiletics. The understated style moves in the direction of naturalness but often results in a carelessness of communication.

The old-school of oratory, on the other hand, has certainly become anachronistic. Neither in politics nor in the church does the William Jennings Bryan-approach wear well.

Yet the principle of effective communication need to be appreciated and appropriated by the preacher, no matter what style happens to fit a particular individual. To speak meaningfully or expressively is more than avoiding a "sing-song" presentation. As the Word begins to speak, even to sing through the preacher, then the sermon takes on a life of its own.

Audible speech and distinct pronunciation are signs of caring, to more than the hearing impaired. Like the body language which is a form of that projection the means of sharing the message are of a piece with the substance.

Conclusion

In a depersonalized age, the preacher will indeed to treat his craft as a soul-touching art. For the pulpit is one of the last places where face-to-face, regular, personalized public communication occurs. The practitioners of preaching will be true to their calling

Preaching as soul-touching Art

as the transcendent Word is sounded in earthy tones and so moves the heart as to make an everyday difference.

The Preaching

Preaching Practice

Acts 20:17-38

This story raises a question—"How do you say goodbye?" In this text the matter is put poignantly. At the end it says that the elders of the church "all wept and embraced Paul and kissed him, sorrowing most of all because of the word he had spoken, that they should see his face no more."

I don't know about you, but I have a hard time with goodbyes. I'm not talking about the daily leave-taking, which is part of the routine at home or at the end of a working-day or after a visit with friends. Rather the sense of awkwardness comes when the farewell is for a long time, for the indefinite future, or forever. Perhaps final farewells bring our mortality too close to the surface for comfort. Whatever the reason, saying goodbye is not easy.

Because all of us need to be able to express ourselves more fully and lovingly I return to this account in Acts. Here Paul is able to give adequate voice to what has gone on between himself and the church at Ephesus.

So it should not be surprising that the whole of what he says pivots around this sentence, "And now, behold, I know that all you among whom I have gone preaching the kingdom of God will see my face no more." His goodbye consists of setting forth those elements of preaching through which he had conveyed his heart and soul to them.

So does this story also provide the occasion to set forth what I see as the essential elements of preaching, believing as I do that any congregation has the need to know where the preacher is coming from and where he or she is heading. I also do this according to the maxim expressed by Richard Baxter, a mentor to many generations of clergy, who stated, "Preach each sermon as if it were your last."

He did not say that with any sense of morbidity, as if fatalistically expecting death. He did so because of the urgency of kingdom come. None of us has forever to make the critical decisions which must be made in this lifetime. Those decisions about what is to have authority and power in our life may come to a head in any given week or day or hour. So no sermon ought to end without that transcendent kingdom becoming immanent in the voice of the preacher and in the heart of the listeners.

Testifying to the Gospel

Preaching the kingdom involves three elements as set forth in this account—testifying to the gospel, declaring the whole counsel of God, and building up the church. It certainly makes sense that the gospel comes first in this list—the good news of the grace of God. For that is the initial picture we have of Jesus himself when he came preaching, "The time is fulfilled, and the kingdom of God is at hand; repent, and believe in the gospel."

The irony of the good news is that it seems to start out seeming so bad. "Repentance" is the term which precedes "grace" in Acts, just as "repent" is the first word out of the mouth of the Lord.

The implicit logic of that sequence of events is that unless you feel the need then proclaiming the love of God will be like "casting pearls before swine." Repentance is like the addict admitting that he or she has lost control of life. Even those with a relatively clean bill of physical and mental health when repenting confess that their life needs changing. Again as Jesus expressed it ironically, "Those without sin have no need of a physician." Or to put it in more recent terms, "The church is a hospital for sinners, not a resort for saints."

Now it happens that we are living in the era of "The Power of Positive Thinking," or as it also has been packaged "The Power of Possibility Thinking." That revolt against "hell, fire and damnation" is understandable. The real world is certainly scary enough without trying to re-kindle old mythologies. Moreover, we are all awakening to a universe which is teeming with creative potential. So why waste time on the seeming negativity of repentance?

The answer of the Great Physician is that the sickness of sin is not an illusion. Therefore when directing yourself to the source of forgiveness, as surely as the flower turns its petals toward the sun's light, then healing begins. The grace of our Lord Jesus Christ comes as company to people in their loneliness, hope to those in despair, and love to those who believe themselves unlovable.

The preaching of the gospel sometimes comes from places other than the pulpit. Presbyterian minister Fred Rogers, of *Mr Rogers' Neighborhood,* has communicated the good news through his children's television program with such lyrics as these:

I like you as you are,
Exactly and precisely.
I think you turned out nicely,
I'll shout it to a star.

That bit of poetry expresses the heart of gospel grace. Even with all our shortcomings and offenses, God accepts us as we are. Or to use Paul's words again, "Even while we were yet sinners, Christ died for us."

Yet, by that same grace, the Lord does not leave us as we are. Rather God enables us to make amends and grow more nearly into his likeness and glory.

The effect of gospel preaching was evident in a phone call from a distant friend lamenting how her mother was subjecting this individual, again, to the "silent treatment." Being displeased by what this family member had done, the parent just quit talking to her.

This now-grown individual is still troubled by what she calls "emotional black-mail." In retrospect, however, she now perceives the pattern of conditional love which has been at work since her childhood. The silent message is "I will love you *if* you do nothing to displease me."

But now, partly in response to gospel-preaching which affirms the "no strings-attached" love of God, she is being strengthened to say "goodbye" to her past anger and depression. Moreover, that preaching was in the setting of a warm church fellowship which make her more accepting of herself, and of others, including her judgmental parent, whom she prays will become whole.

The Whole Counsel

Such prayer brings us to the second element of preaching. Paul speaks of not shrinking from declaring "the whole counsel of God." Beyond the proclamation of the gospel is the application of its meaning to the issues of the day.

The apostle correctly identified the necessity of courage—of not shrinking from this kind of preaching. For on a previous trip to Ephesus he had been charged by the silversmiths with sacrilege. They were idol makers and Paul's preaching was convincing people that gods could not be made by hands. This proved bad for business. So a riot was instigated with the idea of rushing the Christians to judgment. The preacher had gone to "meddlin'."

Since the beginning of Christian preaching, there has been controversy. Indeed, from the time of the Old Testament prophets the "whole counsel" of God has not been limited to so-called spiritual issues. Theologian Karl Barth pictured the preacher as one who had a copy of the Bible in one hand and the daily newspaper in another.

I will never forget the Sunday after President John Kennedy was assassinated. Like other preachers at that time, I was faced with the dilemma of whether such a national tragedy ought to find its way into the content of the sermon the next Sunday.

There was a school of homiletical "purists" who insisted on keeping to their lectionary texts and not deviating from what they had already prepared to say. Certainly I can agree with the notion that sermon content should not be dictated by the latest headlines, lest the sense of transcendental reality beyond all current events be lost.

Yet when an event of such deep and lasting magnitude occurs in the world then ignoring what is on everyone's heart at the moment would be a classic case of avoidance. Of even greater consequence is how the silent treatment leaves people's need to have their grief voiced unmet and their hope restored.

So I departed from the prescribed lesson and instead found one presenting itself for that particular Sunday, which happened also to fall before Thanksgiving Day of 1963. It was the verse from I Thessalonians 5:18 which called for believers to "give thanks in all circumstances." When the whole counsel of God is preached, then the grace of God will be set forth for public as well as private life, in sorrow as well as in joy.

To let go, to say "goodbye" to the past in order to take hold of the future, is not easy. It does not happen without pain and tears—just as the elders wept and embraced Paul on the shores of Ephesius upon his departure. Yet he had prepared them for that last goodbye with the final word he spoke about the preaching he had done in their midst: "Now I commend you to God and to the word of his grace, which is able to build you up..."

Upbuilding the Church

Preaching is certainly a two-way street. It is this final element which distinguishes what happens here in the immediacy of our sanctuary from listening to a sermon on television. The electronic church is remote-control religion. Attempts to worship God in that way have been compared to trying to kiss somebody over the telephone. The relationship is unfulfilling when it does not involve the whole self.

In contrast, the Body of Christ calls forth our participation. Creative listening to a sermon is as active a response as singing a hymn. You put yourself individually into it, not only for what you can take from worship but for the manner in which you let yourself be drawn to one another by the Word. Preaching that upbuilds from this pulpit will offer continuing reflection upon our life together, joining in the common effort to discern where the Lord would lead us in this time and place.

It's been truly said that you may be the only Bible which many people will read. Likewise remember that you may be the only sermons that they may hear. Therefore testify in your daily life to the gospel, declaring the whole counsel of God, and upbuild the church among all who are sanctified.

Social Ministry

The Practice

In Dieter T. Hessel's Preface to his book Social Ministry, he states:

> All church members share one common ministry,
> which is social in all of its aspects.
> Thus there is no question as to whether the
> church will be involved in social ministry;
> the only questions are why and how. As the
> social crisis deepens, will congregations
> retreat from troubling events into quiet
> sanctuaries, or will they become "proactive"
> communities of shalom?

That observation is a valid one. For to do nothing in regard to the world's injustices is, by default, to do something in support of the forces of oppression. *The Deputy*, the play about how the silence of church leadership worsened The Holocaust, is a dramatization of how passivity may be as destructive in effect as active participation in evil.

Mandate

Moreover, for persons of the Judeo-Christian faith tradition, there is no avoiding the mandates of the Hebrew prophets. While Jesus led no political movement, his kingdom teaching and mighty works were experienced as a threat to the status quo by the power and principalities of that time.

In the intervening centuries churches have often become the bastion of the status quo, thereby resisting the biblical mandate of letting "justice roll down like the waters, and righteousness like an everflowing stream." The Crusades and The Inquisition were examples of ecclesiastical power being used for inhumane purposes.

Yet in each generation, spokespersons arise to challenge inequities, like the "Presbyterian Rebellion," as the Revolutionary War was called in 18th century America. Clergyman John Witherspoon was a signer of The Declaration of Independence. Slavery was abolished in 19th century Britain in large measure because of Methodist influence, and in the United States because of the combined efforts of various faith groups. The civil rights struggle and Vietnam War were occasions for the development of 20th century movements within the religious community.

More recently, witness and ministry inspired by Liberation Theology have spread beyond South America. Interfaith advocacy groups have arisen to lobby for humanitarian legislation. Among these is Bread for the World, which was originally headed by Lutheran pastor Arthur Simon, who has written, "a single action by Congress or one decision by the President can undo—or multiply—many times over the effect of all voluntary contributions combined." From the Catholic and conservative Protestant communities have come fervent Pro-Life efforts to end abortion.

Resistance

Yet the very range of commitments across the ideological spectrum suggests why local congregations are reluctant to become socially active. Because a given church or synagogue is likely to be composed of persons with a wide diversity of political views, clergy find that there is a decided limit in staking out controversial positions on controversial issues. "The egg hits the fan" particularly in cases where denominational bodies make social pronouncements which appear to speak for individual members or congregations.

When advocacy is added to the social ministry mix, then the likelihood of conflict is increased. Lobbying for changes in public policy doesn't seem to be a legitimate religious activity to the average person in the pew. What is one person's advocacy is another's "meddling." If benevolence funds are budgeted to such causes, necks are apt to turn even redder.

So from the standpoint of many faith communities, following the old adage that "religion and politics don't mix" seems to be the prudent course. While this is undoubtedly the safest alternative, our faith mandates that we not "bury our head in the sand." In a media-driven era, with Martin Luther King, Jr., having been on one end of the spectrum, and Pat Robertson now on the other, it is unrealistic for clergy to ignore the forces which are giving shape to the future our nation and the world.

Guidelines

So the question is how clergy are to fulfill their prophetic role responsibly, while fostering the consensus upon which every voluntary organization depends. That balancing act is a challenge, to say the least. The following guidelines represent the ways this pastor has sought to respond creatively to the biblical mandate, despite the resistance to addressing the vital social issues of our day.

1. Preach and teach forthrightly on controversial issues, but not incessantly, nor in a dogmatic tone. It is important for the preacher not to have just one string on his violin, nor to purport to speak infallibly on social concerns. In addition, showing how public and private faith practice is all an expression of the same spirituality is a "must."

2. Serve as a broker for those desiring to become involved in social action. Clergy ought to be able to refer people to advocacy groups. Over the years I have been pleased to help individuals get connected with everything from Operation Breadbasket in Chicago to the ecumenical Texas Impact, which advocates for human services before the state legislature.

3. Let the ministry of social services support the social action impetus. Those members whose call it is to be hands–on, as in working with Habitat for Humanity or with the Interfaith

Hospitality Network, may be led to probe the underlying reasons for the shortage of housing for lower income and for the plight of the homeless. The Good Samaritan parable implies that discipleship will lead to addressing the causes of violence, as well as binding up the wounds of victims left beside the road.

A Case Study

For a three year period during my ministry, I served as an elected high school board member. Because I made it clear to my congregation that I was running for the office as a citizen and concerned parent rather than as a clergyperson, members of the church were able to appreciate my civic involvement.

As it happened, during two of those years, when I was serving as president of the board, a controversy arose about prayers in school. It was in the midst of that debate that I had opportunity to work with a constitutional lawyer who was retained by the board to advise its members on policies relating to religious practices on public property.

Based on that experience I wrote articles on the subject for both educational and religious journals, including one for *The Clergy Journal* entitled, "Invocations in a Pluralistic Society" (April 1987). I concluded that the appropriate form which such exercises should take in a secular setting is either to call for a moment of silence, or to provide a meditation into which both prayerful and non-prayerful persons are free to impute their own meanings. An example of that form is the invocation which I presented before The Texas House of Representatives.

> As this legislative body prepares itself for the proceedings of the day, I would bid you to do so in a meditative spirit...some with eyes open, some with them closed, but with all called upon to be open a Higher Power from which to draw inspiration and courage...lest we forget that it is only as we lose our life for the sake of the common good that we find it for ourselves, as each in his or her own way says, Amen.

The following is a sermon which also seeks to apply the guidelines in name of the one who embodied the rule of truth.

The Preaching

RULE OF TRUTH

John 18:32-37

Christ the King Sunday—before Thanksgiving Day

This story leaves us hanging with the question, "What is truth?" It is one which theologians and philosophers have had a field day with over the centuries. But it was by no means an academic debate in which that question was posed.

Rather it was asked in the midst of the life and death situation which led to the crucifixion. The question came from the Roman governor as a result of highly charged political intrigue and deception.

The Truth Question

But let us take careful note of how there was a preceding question in the story, the one which provides the basis for resolving the second issue. I'm referring to the initial query, "Are you the King of the Jews?"

Jesus' initial reply was, in effect, that the accusations fell of their own weight. If he had assumed such a title, his followers would have been doing battle to keep him from being delivered over. Pilate knew that there had been no such resistance to the arrest.

So Pilate's asking "What is truth?" is not so much a question as a sigh of despair. You feel like he'd like to know. But he had one ear cocked to the crowd outside. They put the squeeze on him further by threatening, "If you release this man, you are not Caesar's friend; every one who makes himself a king sets himself over Caesar." That threat turned the tide. Pilate would not jeopardize his own position by letting rumor get back to the Emporer that he was soft on alleged traitors. So he had Jesus delivered up. Truth, it seemed, took a beating—no, a crucifixion, again.

Yet the irony is that the one who thought he was in control was being controlled. The supreme irony was that the one over whom he had power was much more in command of the situation, having so selected the circumstances for his trial that those who would be his judge were themselves being judged. So much in command was Jesus that later generations would sing of him "King of Kings and Lord of Lords."

The Truth "Will Out"

How the rule of truth holds sway, how the truth "will out" is evident in these conclusions drawn by historian Charles Beard after tracking the saga of the human story:

> Whom the gods would destroy, they first make mad with power.
> The bee fertilizes the flower which it would rob.
> The night is darkest before the dawn.

Only a few years ago the world witnessed the crumbling of the Berlin Wall as the most visible sign that communist powers had proved bankrupt. Certainly the demise of authoritarian regimes is evidence that no rule endures without responsiveness to the needs of all people, without their being included in the decision-making process, and that ultimately power has to be in conformity with reality which no official lie can conceal indefinitely. While at no time did Christ exercise his sovereignty by force, every principality has had eventually to submit itself to those Christ-like truths or perish.

Holding Sway Today

But the truth question is no less ours to answer than it has been for those in other times and places. "The strife of truth with falsehood," in the lyrics of James Russell Lowell, is one which comes to mind on this Sunday before the great national day of

Thanksgiving. The gratitude we are meant to feel is for the truth represented by our Pilgrim forebears.

We should remember that persons who named themselves Separatists came to this country to practice the truth of their conscience. In their homeland they were, in their own words, "hunted and persecuted on every side" by those seeking to make them Conformists within the established church. So they separated themselves out and fled across the sea from state-imposed religion.

Thomas Jefferson was similarly inspired when he spoke of "The Wall of Separation" between church and state. Those who visit his graveside at Charlottesville, Virginia will find etched on his tombstone the three things he wanted most to be remembered for. Not one of these had to do with his being President of the United States. Rather the remembrances were for having penned the Declaration of Indepedence, for the founding of the University of Virginia, and for authoring the Statute of Religious Liberty, which contained the provision separating church and state.

Thus was a distinctively American interpretation given to Jesus' words, "My kingdom is not of this world." Particularly are we as citizens not only of this Republic but of God's kingdom as well meant to defend and maintain that "Wall of Separation" in an era when that precious heritage is under assault. Televangelists-turned-politicians have, among others, launched attacks upon the doctrine.

The Rule in School

For us the question of protecting and pursuing the truth, and affirming the rule of truth is being posed in the Prayer in School debate. Prayer has, God forbid, become "a political football." Let it be noted for all to remember that thirty years ago when the Supreme Court ruled that prescribed prayer had no place in the public schools of a pluralistic society, the General Assembly of the United Presbyterian Church, U.S.A. supported that interpretation of the Bill of Rights.

Certainly both the Court and that church body affirmed the necessity of teaching *about* religion in the schools, because there is no separating faith traditions from the civilizations and cultures to which they have given shape. But as former Senator Lowell Weicker who opposed one of the many attempts to offer a constitutional amendment declared, "Not only would so-called voluntary prayer pressure children and youth to conform, it is not even necessary. For as long as there are algebra tests, there will be prayers in school."

His point is well taken. Moreover, you and I are called upon to guard and defend the sanctity of prayer from all who would misuse or abuse what is meant to be that most precious relationship with God through our Lord Jesus Christ. In a land where there are soon to be more Muslims than Presbyterians, for the sake of being true to our own convictions, as well as those of others, we will resist any attempts to water-down prayer, in the futile search for some elusive common-denominator.

For within the inner sanctum of our souls, neither Pilate nor Caesar nor the United States Congress has any more business than in the privacy of our homes. Neither the schools nor the state ought in any way to assume the form of a church. For it is within the intimacy of communion with our Heavenly Parent, and with our brothers and sisters in the Body of Christ that each of us comes to obey the rule of truth in our lives and are able to sing of him, "King of kings and Lord of lords, and he shall reign forever and ever."

Stewardship

The Practice

"When it comes to giving to the church, some people will stop at nothing!"

This bit of humor was something I remember from a conference on stewardship I attended over twenty years ago. The event was called DISC—Dimensions of Stewardship Commitment. It was one of two resources provided by my denomination which has proved especially useful in parish practice. The guidelines delineated below draw from that DISC training.

The other resource was a definition which continues to work well. I have converted that summary statement into the following responsive reading, used annually in the service preceding the dedication of pledges.

Leader: What is Christian Stewardship?

People: It is the systematic and proportionate giving of time, talent, and material possessions.

Leader: Upon what is this giving based?

People: It is based on the conviction that these resources are a trust from God.

Leader: What is the motive for sharing these resources?

People: The motive is gratitude for Christ's redeeming love.

Leader: Toward what end are these resources to be used?

People: They are to be used in God's service that his kingdom may come in this place and throughout the earth.

Such a comprehensive understanding of what constitutes this commitment is a necessary starting point. Otherwise giving patterns are apt to be haphazard.

Specifics beyond generalities, however, are needed in the cultivation of responsible sharing. In this regard I know of no substitute for a the development of an annual theme which incorporates forthcoming goals of the congregation. The realization of these aims is thereby shown to be dependent upon generous support.

The Theme/Team

Sometimes the theme presents itself in terms of a very clear need. When a capital improvement program was necessary, including the lighting of the church steeple, then "Let Your Light Shine" emerged as a central concept. It arose, as most themes will, from a scriptural source, in this case Matthew 5:16.

Inseparable from the theme is the creation of a logo which enables people to visualize the aspiration. This process has proved to be most successful when the design comes from the interaction of congregational members. A drawing serves to unify the stewardship program, from its imprint on the pledge card to providing the brochure/bulletin covers and banner design for Stewardship Commitment Sunday.

The cooperative effort of a planning groups is indispensable, and often becomes a worthy end in itself,as well as being a means to an end. For instance, good fellowship is generated in putting together a set of Sunday afternoon neighborhood teas where lay leaders interpret the stewardship goals. Smaller group gatherings frequently prove to be a fruitful means of relating because they allow for give–and–take. There is also a place for presentations in larger settings to stir enthusiasm for special projects.

A brochure is essential for interpretation, for use both in gatherings and through mailings. In addition to spelling out the particualr objectives for the year, this written piece serves as the vehicle for explaining the importance of pledging—without which there is no reliable planning. "Giving as the Spirit moves" may be a conviction held sincerely, but it also may serve as a rationalization for carelessness in giving.

Also this publication can provide the rationale for how one annual commitment is a far more responsible way to support the church than through "nickeling and dimeing" people a multitude of fund–raisers. "Putting all your 'begs' in one 'askit'" is a memorable way of expressing that truth.

As the procurement of pledges follows the interpretative phase of the program, the issue of "The Every Member Canvas" arises. In recent years that once-common practice of recruiting callers has given way to a mailing by which time and talent service opportunities are presented, as well as including a pledge card.

The approach by mail is effective provided that it is preceded by a year-around process of interpretation and an on-going attention to the climate of the congregation, a dimension requiring separate treatment. Moreover, a team follow-up on the third of a congregation which usually does not respond initially is necessary.

A phone call or personal visit is then in order, as individuals are apt to forget. The personal contact also allows for possible grievances to be aired—feelings sometimes not evident until a financial decision is at hand. Pastoral care can then be directed to persons needing attention. The degree of unhappiness depends as much, however, on the atmosphere within the congregation as does it does on economic or personal issues.

The Climate

This factor, though coming last in the sequence of elements, is by no means least. Indeed without such a nurturing context, not much can be expected to happen as far as persons' self-giving is concerned. That truth derives from the fact that personal sharing is motivated by feeling even more than reason. So a positive feeling-tone which manifests itself outside the stewardship season is what leads people to go the extra-mile in terms of extending themselves time, talent and money-wise.

How giving "happens" in such a setting was particularly evident in the initiative taken by an individual who was not even a parishioner but who had been exposed to the lively spirit of a growing church. When the pastor responded to this person's invitation to visit, he learned of a $19,000 "out-of-the-blue" gift to fund the paving of a church parking lot.

Another sign of support has come through bequests, which in one instance resulted in a $300,000 remembrance of the church. While earnings from large endowment funds may in some instances have caused individual contributors to conclude that their giving was not neccesary, that consequence need not be the case. Properly used and interpreted, such funds can provide incentive for greater support. Indeed, leading development consultants have predicted that unless any given non–profit institution makes provision for a growing endowment for mission and operating expenses by the end of this century, it will not get far into the next century.

While unexpected acts of great generosity may not seem a common occurrence, they will prove less uncommon than many might expect as opportunities are provided to meet people-needs even more than property-needs. When a "multiplier-effect" can be shown to happen, as even a child's offering can provide a chick through the Heifer Project, which in turn leads to the sharing of many other chicks, then stewardship is both caught and taught.

Of the various contributors to the total stewardship process, the pastor sets the tone in a variety of ways. Preaching provides the particular focus to that leadership, as sermons continually highlight the spirit and substance of self-giving. The following homily suggests something of how congregants may be led not to stop at nothing when it comes to their giving.

The Preaching

GOD'S BELONGINGS

Matthew 22: 15-22

I am sure that you recognize this as one of the most frequently quoted passages in the Bible. The reason is that it's the one place where Jesus seems to express himself most clearly about the relation of church and state, a subject of interest to us all.

Yet this text also provides insight into the meaning of stewardship. That emphasis is evident in the latter part of his answer: "Render to God the things that are God's."

The Meaning of Stewardship

For what is it that belongs to God? Only religious paraphernalia? Churches, hymn books, rosary beads? Of course not! As the Psalmist declares, "The earth is the Lord's and the fullness thereof..." In other words, everything belongs to God.

Therefore, to render to God is to give one's whole self to the Lord, while rendering only a fraction of the self to Caesar. Consequently, loyalty to the earthly ruler is made subservient to the obedience to the heavenly ruler. In a broader sense, the teaching takes us beyond the relationship of church and state to God's relation to the whole of life.

If "The earth is the Lord's..." then it will affect our attitude toward to all that we call our belongings. Our notion of ownership itself will change as we awaken to how we are but stewards, trustees of everything—from our institutions of government to our use of land and water, from the houses to which we hold title to the persons whom we call our family.

This truth found striking confirmation in a correspondence between a New York law firm and one in New Orleans. The Louisiana attorneys were asked to trace the title of a given parcel to as early a date as possible. Upon returning information which reported ownership dating to 1803, a further inquiry was sent from New York asking for still an earlier date. The following reply was mailed:

> Gentleman: Please be advised that in the year 1803 the United States of America acquired the territory of Louisiana from the French Republic by purchase. The Republic of France, in turn, acquired title from the Spanish Crown by conquest. The Spanish Crown had obtained it by virtue of one Christopher Columbus, a Genoese sailor who had been authorized to embark by Queen Isabella of Spain, who obtained sanction from the Pope, the Vicar of Christ, who is the Son and heir of Almighty God, who made Louisiana!

That does, indeed, seem to follow the origin back just about as far as you can go. It also helps us grasp the sense of how the blessings of the Creator have been showered upon us, as we have been entrusted with the gifts of creation; and how in Christ, through the gift of re-creation we have been the recipients of a generosity beyond reckoning.

The Exercise of Stewardship

But the transition from this theory of stewardship to the practice of it is no simple matter. In fact, we begin our days with the fundamental need for a sense of ownership.

When you read about ages and stages in child psychology, you learn that you don't begin with sharing. "Good Christian" instincts to the contrary, you begin with letting the toddler get firm hold of whatever it is that seems important to claim, without urging him or her to share it with someone else. Any forced charity just meets up with resistance. Until our insecurities are dealt with, our sense of ownership confirmed, there is no basis for sharing. You can't give away what you don't have.

So from childhood on, the element of ownership is vital to personal and social health. That would be the end of the matter, except for the words which come ringing down the years "...render unto God the things that are God's." That is a jarring note as we confront the dilemma of how to reconcile my list of assets—real and personal property, stocks, bonds, IRAs, cars, VCRs with the claim that "The earth is the Lord's and the fullness thereof."

Part of the answer is fear. If the wrath of God seems an anachronism, consider the ozone layer. If humans do not forsake the illusion that we can do with the earth's resources just as we please, then we will lose the protection which surrounds the planet.

Yet the willingness to let go of selfish habits does not arise simply out of fear, but from models of inspiration, who show how you can only keep what you let go of. In this regard there is none to compare with the one who suffered the loss of all things for our sake.

When it comes to making the decision about the disposition of our own resources, may it be that we discern how stewardship is not a matter of how much we give to the church, but how we spend all of our money—indeed the whole of our lives. It has truly been said that you can tell more about people's faith by the stubs in their check book than by the number of hymns they can sing by heart.

That's indeed music to our ears, by one who prompts us to share freely by his own enduring self-sacrifice. Let us so do knowing that "...all things are yours—the present or the future, all are yours; and you are Christ's; and Christ is God's."

Storytelling

The Practice

Storytelling—is it a luxury or necessity in the life of faith? As with all the arts in society, storytelling seems more ornamental than fundamental.

Yet the opposite is true when viewed from the standpoint of *The Greatest Story Ever Told,* as Christians have come to identify the life of Christ. Jesus himself was a master storyteller, as is evident in his parables, continuing as they do the tradition of the Hebrew scriptures.

Moreover, he became the inspiration for the storytelling impulse in all subsequent generations of believers. Whether it was Augustine of Hippo in his unprecedented autobiography *The Confessions* or John Bunyan in his *Pilgrim's Progress* or more recently C.S. Lewis and Madeline L'Engle in their fictional writings, persons of faith have quickened the imagination in a way that abstract doctrine cannot match. Even though the left-brain analysis of Narrative Theology has thrown light on the subject, it is the daily practice of storytelling, an essentially right-brain activity which enlivens and enriches ministry.

Whence arises that power of truth in fiction or of real-life tales which are stranger than fiction?

The Power

Every preacher knows that illustrations engage people's attention and heart in a way which "gets under the skin" of listeners, as the story engenders empathetic identification and reaches subliminal depths. Our stories shape us fully as much as we shape them.

That influence is particularly visible in family relations. As stories of forebears are passed from one generation to the next, descendants are reminded of origins and may be inspired with a sense of destiny. Holidays frequently become the occasion for recounting not only long-ago formative events but also first-hand experiences which have made a critical difference to them and their loved ones.

But even in the broader culture, we are able to recognize how pervasive is storytelling. Television has rightly been called a "Storytelling Box." News stories, soap operas, the beautiful and banal are everywhere and always "on the air" around us.

Stories of the self pour forth from the mouths of children telling of their day in school, of salesmen regaling customers, of patients on psychiatrists' couches, of participants in Twelve-Step meetings around the world, of the elderly who replay the past. Storytelling is a natural expression for persons of all conditions and ages. The power of stories is also apparent in the variety of uses to which they are put—to amuse, challenge, inform, motivate, and reveal the mystery beyond words.

Uses

Within the religious community storytelling takes on a wide variety of forms for a multitude of purposes in preaching, teaching, and ministering. The recent spate of books on the subject reflects a growing appreciation of the need to be aware of stories as an indispensable element in spirituality.

It was when commencing ministry in the southern part of the United States, where storytelling is intrinsic to the culture, that I was introduced to the practice of both clergy and laity recounting their "faith journeys" as a way of opening themselves to others. I must confess to having had some reservation upon entering into that process. In the age of Donahue and Oprah, the "tell all" syndrome threatens to trivialize what should be the most intimate and precious of life experiences. Yet when done appropriately, a sharing of personal experiences enhances mutual understanding and appreciation.

Even in such mundane settings as a church business meeting, a light story fittingly told can "break the ice" or move people into a more creative frame of mind. Certainly in calling and counseling, pastors are in position more often to listen than to tell stories, as persons are hungry for another to "hear them out."

But when in the telling mode, clergy will best serve their parishioners by communicating their stories skillfully. Indeed, the skill in the telling of them may become as important as the substance of the narrative.

Skills

Certainly the principles in the art of storytelling transcend any religious use. Aristotle's *Poetics* and *Rhetoric* still provide valid guidelines when it comes to a story having a beginning, a middle, and end, with no extraneous elements, and with its building to a climax and having a cathartic effect.

Yet within the faith community, stories need to include a spiritual dimension. William J. Bausch in his book *STORYTELLING Imagination and Faith* offers helpful suggestions of method, in terms of learning, owning, contemplating, sharing and celebrating the story.

Moreover, pastors have to be especially careful not to become "preachy" in their storytelling. Better to leave the "moral of the story" to the listeners' imagination rather than "hitting them over the head" with it. Truly has it been said that good stories are not meant to be confused with Western Union telegrams. Jesus made marvelous use of the open-ended story, as the Parable of the Prodigal Son well illustrates. Does the elder brother heed the father's assurance, or continue in bitter spirit? Indeed it's left for each of us to decide.

It's been with these principles in mind that I have found stories presenting themselves periodically as extended illustrations in sermons. While use of narrative should by no means be overdone in expository preaching, there are occasions when a story may comprise most, if not all, of the sermon.

I have found Christmas Eve to be one of those times. For carols and candles create a particularly receptive climate. I offer one example of a story which presented itself to me in that right-brain state of consciousness between wakefulness and sleep, which I subsequently presented on a night before Christmas.

The Preaching

Saving Dream

It was Christmas Eve. Joseph was all alone. After years of working to isolate himself, he had succeeded all too well. "The pursuit of happiness" meant being his own man. He was good at his business, a self-confessed workaholic, being married to his job; at least that's what his ex-wife had claimed on the day of their divorce.

She was right, of course; and if he had been honest, he would have made the break before the children came. As far as he was concerned, those three kids had grown up orphans, so little had their father been around. Now that their mother had remarried and taken them elsewhere, Christmas was little more than an exchange of parcel post packages.

Maybe it was these boxes, sitting lifelessly on the kitchen table which triggered the loneliness which had been accumulating over the past months like a non-stop snow fall. He never thought solitude could constrict his throat and cause a drowsiness which felt like the depression-induced sleep he had heard about.

Then it seemed that he "came to" with the fright of a panic attack. So in an effort to find diversion, he picked up the newspaper, and his eye fell almost immediately upon an advertised phone number for people to call when they were alone at Christmas, a church-sponsored Yule-Connection.

He mused to himself, "This looks like a hot-line for misfits." Nevertheless, he found his finger dialing the number. Before he was quite aware what he had done, a voice was on the line. It was that of woman who said simply, "May I help you?"

He paused, as he wrestled with the impulse to hang up but blurted instead, "I just wanted somebody to talk to."

"You're feeling lonely," she replied.

"I didn't expect to," he continued. "Oh, I can understand why some people would want to use your services, because they're too old or poor. But actually I've wanted to be by myself."

"But now you are feeling differently," said the voice at the other end.

"Well, I wouldn't be on the line if I didn't. But I still don't understand why I'm telling you all this, even at Christmas. It never amounted to anything in our home. My mother died before I scarcely knew what Christmas trees were; and my father didn't believe in them anyway. So I didn't need them."

"What," she queried, "the trees or your parents?"

"Neither,really," he asserted. "I've been a self-made man all my life. I might as well not have had parents."

"Your father didn't support you?"

"Of course he did."

"Your mother didn't do anything more than give you birth?'

At this point, it seemed like an avalanche gave way within him. His voice cracked as he answered, "I have only a dim recollection of her, calling me by a name that no one else used. I remember standing by her grave; that was maybe the only time I've ever cried."

But it was not the last time he was to weep. To his consternation he began to sob, uncontrollably, for a full five minutes. It was all he could do to hold the receiver in his hand.

When the tears began to subside, he heard the voice say, "You have to cry sometimes. It seems there is no joy apart from grief. So instead of saying `Merry Christmas,' I would bring to you `good news of a great joy.' Good night, Joey dearest."

The line went dead on the other end. He still held the phone's cradle in his hand in disbelief. It wasn't the abrupt ending to the conversation that took him back but what she had called him—"Joey dearest."

How did she know that? This had been an anonymous call. But not only did she know he was Joseph but knew the nickname which only his mother had used. Once the initial shock passed, he quickly redialed the number.

Again a shock: this time he got a recorded message, "The number you have called has been disconnected."

Immediately he dialed Information,reported the puzzle. The operator replied, "You know, that is puzzling. People have been trying that number all night; but the sponsoring churches had to disconnect because they couldn't find volunteers to take the calls. I can't imagine who it could have been you were talking to."

As he replaced the receiver, Joe's premonition was confirmed. The fact that it had been a woman's voice is what may have obscured the miraculous sense that he was in contact with One who knew him better than he knew himself.

Suddenly Joseph did in fact awake, from what had been a dream of a call from beyond. Now he knew that not another Christmas would pass when a Hot-Line would be lacking his willingness to volunteer.

Teamwork

The Practice

The original title of this article was going to be "Staff." That subject seemed a logical one in a series on parish practice which has included such other topics as Administration and Stewardship.

Yet upon further reflection, I concluded that "Teamwork" is the better choice of terms. For that dimension of ministry encompasses the full range of cooperative efforts, of which staff relationships is but one component. Moreover, not all congregations have staffs, but all must have teamwork if the purpose of faith community is to be achieved.

Nevertheless, including staff issues in these reflections will provide a perspective helpful in considering the other variety of relationships. For what happens in the interaction among paid professionals illustrates what applies to all members of a team in regard to the "Three R's" of Teamwork: Reciprocity, Respect, Reward.

Reciprocity

Discerning the heart of a reciprocal relationship, whereby benefits are shared between parties, is a fitting starting point. Sometimes it is assumed that wherever there is supervision such mutual give and take is impossible. It seems like the Pope in the College of Cardinals—that association being described as one in which "All may be created equal; but some are more equal than others." Yet the necessity of supervision, whether it is in a solo pastorate where a Staff Committee oversees the work of a minister or of a multiple staff where a Senior Pastor supervises the work of others—that necessity is not at variance with collegiality. All stand to learn from others in the spirit of shared ministry.

For instance, after twenty five years of supervising seminary students in their field work and internships I have come to regard these younger folks as colleagues. Certainly I was able to mentor them, drawing upon my experience to help them "learn the ropes." But I have cherished what they had to teach in helping me keep in touch with what is going on in a fast-changing world.

So it is too that clergy and laity may enjoy the special talents which they bring to one another. Martin Luther's "Priesthood of All Believers" catches the spirit of that interaction. Lay people are in a daily position to exercise the stewardship of the gospel in a way not even approximated by the circumstances of clergy. Non-ordained participants in Twelve Step groups are probably serving as more effective instruments of healing throughout the general population than the "religious professionals."

So reciprocity may be perceived as that miraculous element in teamwork which "divides our griefs and multiplies our joys." That give and take in sharing the means of grace is inseparable from the second element of teamwork.

Respect

As in a marriage, respect is an aspect of teamwork which takes on particular significance in the religious community. Just how vital a role respect plays may be discerned when it is not present. If a minister believes that he or she is meant to coach, cover all bases and sell the tickets besides, then that person and his or her congregation are in trouble. That compulsion implies little trust in what lay persons could and should do. Or when "professional laypersons" try to tell the clergy how to do their jobs, then the tension becomes like that in a dysfunctional family where members and clergy find themselves "walking on eggshells."

Essential to maintaining due respect among paid staff is for each congregation to formulate written staff policies. Position descriptions clarify tasks, a simple procedure which fosters good morale. Spelling out work conditions, from holidays to sick leave, helps objectify what may become bones of contention otherwise.

Even though borrowed from secular personnel practices, having a Staff Committee is certainly consistent with the biblical emphasis on accountability. Jesus' parables on stewards who have oversight of households, and of owners who have comparable oversight over stewards implicitly support exercising authority with all due respect. Moreover clergy, instead of being threatened by laity whom they may feel are "looking over their shoulder," should welcome the input which comes only through candid interchange. When the fundamental context is one of support, then the third essential element of teamwork comes clearly into play.

Reward

Appreciation may be an even more appropriate word for that aspect of teamwork than reward. For this element applies across the board, whether among paid staff, or between clergy and laity.

None of this is to imply that fair pay is to be underestimated in importance in regard to professionals. "Raise me, don't praise me!" was what a business friend of mine used to say. He thereby emphasized that anyone working for slave wages was likely to be less than enthusiastic about the task. Yet even when adequate compensation is assured, or when among volunteers compensation is not an issue, the reward factor is always a necessity.

One psychologist of note has observed that the underlying cause of stress and burn-out on the job is not having too much work to do nor even in having too little time to do it. More often it has to do with lack of appreciation. And while no one is meant to do what they do for the sake of recognition, everyone needs "strokes." No wonder those in the trophy business do so well! They are providing services to meet a very basic human need.

Certainly teamwork in the church depends upon good morale no less than on the playing field. That process is an agreement in advance upon what it means to win in a given situation, a clear notion of the role which each of the participants is meant to play, and provision for celebrating team victories. The following sermon suggests that the whole of our life together in ministry is intended to show forth such meaning of partnership.

The Preaching

PARTNERS

Philippians 1:1-11

I would enter into partnership with you as we are led to think about partners. This association is made here in this text as Paul wrote how he was "...thankful for the partnership in the gospel" with the faithful in the church at Philippi.

It helps to know that he was remembering his shared ministry with them from the confines of a prison cell in Rome. He wrote this letter to those in the church which he had helped start years before in the Macedonian community and with whom he had the sense of continuing kinship. For they had remembered him in his affliction, having sent a gift by the hand of one Ephaphroditus, whom they had also sent to remain with Paul as a servant.

Moreover, toward the end of this letter Paul uses that same word again as he recalls, "...when I left Macedonia, no church entered into partnership with me in giving and receiving except you only."

The Vision

It is also instructive to note that the Greek word he used in describing that relationship was *koinonia*—most often translated "fellowship" in the eighteen other places it appears in the New Testament. Originally that term meant a business association, as we speak today of partnerships in a legal sense.

Certainly there is no minimizing the extent to which the economic factor enters into any meaningful community. That's clearly the case in marriage where *koinonia* is inseparable from sharing materially. Yet we know that the intimacy of the home is at-risk when the sharing becomes more a matter of dollars and cents than of affection, of common values, of love.

Recently I had occasion to learn how the uniqueness of the Christian community continued to evidence itself over the centuries, particularly in regard to music. I had long puzzled about why the major scale emerged in European culture, while only the minor scale is to be found in all other societies. It seems that the monks of the Middle Ages started singing together in a new way, for the first time in parts. So it is that chords and harmony developed with new, major intervals evolving in that communal setting.

After seeing the delightful musical *Nunsense*, however, I wonder whether that innovation was no less a gift of women than of men. For one set of lyrics included the line, "Just a couple of nuns learning to sing in harmony."

Whatever its origin, harmony can be taken as representing cooperation in a broader and deeper sense, thereby suggesting what partnership may mean within and beyond the church. *Koinonia* continues to provide the vision in a world which forever is seeking to tear down "the ties that bind our hearts in Christian love."

The Challenge

Of course, the vision was never fulfilled even in biblical times. The people then were not walking around with halos over their heads any more than we are. In fact it was the bickering which was going on in the church at Philippi which occasioned Paul's writing of this letter.

The challenge in each generation since the time of Christ has been to redefine that partnership in ever changing circumstances. In our present era that sense of comity has taken a particularly hard beating as evidenced in the outbreak of civil disorder. Urban riots have left us all painfully aware of how limited and uneven has been our progress since the last round of violence.

Suddenly we are awakening to how cooperation is essential to our survival as a nation. It has been observed that there are two particular government officials who have best interpreted how the breakdown is not so much of law and order as of the underlying community ties. It is no accident that both of these people were former professional athletes. One is Democratic Senator from New Jersey Bill Bradley, who once played with the New York Knicks basketball team. The other is former Republican Urban Affairs cabinet member Jack Kemp, who played football with the Buffalo Bills. It happens that athletics may be the place where fellowship is most nearly approximated in the public arena.

Globally we find ourselves on spaceship earth where all former notions of nations being able to go-it-alone are giving way to an ecological consciousness. Such awareness was evident in regard to the Earth Summit recently held in Rio de Janeiro. A senior UN advisor was quoted as saying, "We're talking about a new partnership. I hope Rio is going to be a good beginning."

Toward Partnership

Yet slow as the movement may be toward partnership, we need to pray that the change proves to be inexorable, because the only alternative is self-destruction. It is truly a life and death struggle for ourselves and our children.

So I would share with you contemporary images which imply what partnership in Christ may mean for the future. One of these is far away, the other closer to home.

About as far as people can get is in outer space where the world once observed in wonder via TV how astronauts could bring a wandering satellite into the cargo bay of their spaceship. The spectacle of a single human able to manipulate a multi-ton capsule is enough to boggle our minds, a visual counterpart to the faith which can move mountains. But what made this recent venture beyond the atmosphere so moving was to witness the way these three persons worked together to retrieve the stray satellite. That spatial feat is sign of hope for breakthroughs in earthly cooperation.

Back on earth, in the midst of the billion dollar wreckage of the Los Angeles riots several years ago, the cleanup promised new and creative partnerships. Residents immediately began donating food and clothes to those left destitute. Spontaneous broom and shovel brigades were formed. Enclaves of all colors and creeds reached out to one another. Such response to catastrophe may yet serve as a catalyst to get all segments of the nation to act in concert to address the causes of social unrest: the joblessness, the poor housing, health care, education.

The partnership of practice and prayer is as much ours today as it was for Paul and his friends in Philippi. Let us, therefore, like them become partakers of that same grace, "filled with the fruits of righteousness which come through Jesus Christ."

Weddings

The Practice

"Why do you want to get married in the church?" That is the question I pose to each couple who asks to be married in the church, whether the two are members of the congregation or not. Having a judge officiate at the exchange of wedding vows is certainly as legal as having a clergy person conducting the ceremony. So focusing upon the distinctive purpose of a wedding service in the sanctuary helps partners think about the spiritual dimension of the relationship.

It is certainly not enough to say that a church wedding is customary, as if a bride wouldn't "feel married" unless walking down an aisle. That attitude assumes the wedding service as only so much "frosting on the cake," not part of the ingredients itself. Such superficiality replays the too common "hatched, matched and dispatched" practice of religion in Europe, with people so often attending worship only at baptisms, weddings and funerals.

Reflecting the Marriage

The integrity of the forthcoming marriage itself should be reflected in the wedding. When one promises unconditional love to the other, in sorrow as well as in joy, in sickness as well as in health, in want as well as in plenty, and not just as long as each feels like it but for a lifetime—that commitment requires so much of people they need to feel the need for help in fulfilling the vow. To speak the vows under the Cross is to affirm God's availability as a silent partner in the union to supply the grace necessary to fulfill them. To speak the vows in the company of believers is to receive the assurance of that support group which is the church.

Officiating clergy serve a special function in that community, but by no means encompasses it. At best, the pre-marital counseling between pastor and couple will heighten awareness of the extended family function which a congregation is meant to play.

The pre-marital meetings commence the process when the pastor invites a continuing relationship with the prospective bride and groom. Such continuity implies that the partners are either members of the church, or are in some way involved in its life. Some churches have adopted explicit policies stating that wedding ceremonies are limited to members. My procedure has been to invite strangers who phone, requesting wedding services, to identify themselves after a Sunday morning worship, at which time appointment can be made to discuss the possibility. As simple a prerequisite as that separates many a sheep from the goats, maritally speaking.

Another requirement is that each partner complete a questionnaire which lifts up aspects of the relationship, particularly in areas of particular conflict. Better to flag these ahead of time than to wait until after the fact. The Methodists have produced a marriage manual which contains such a form. A follow–up interview to the wedding, which I express in terms of a "10,000 mile checkup or a year, whichever comes first," is part of the process. One ingenious pastor charged $150 to every couple whom he married, but promised a "refund" if they came back for such a checkup after a year!

I also invite the couple to write what they would like to have me incorporate in a meditation which would give expression to their union. I explain that while for generations 1 Corinthinans 13 and other texts have been used for weddings, theirs is a unique relationship for which the scripture has special meaning. So I am prepared to say in their behalf what they would like others to hear as to how they love each other.

Wedding Procedures

The wedding ceremony procedures certainly ought not to be slighted. A printed booklet placed in the hands of a couple before the first interview provides much of that important information. How to obtain a license, the church policies governing fees, photographers, (e.g. no flash pictures during the worship service), the range of musical selections, an outline of the service, of receiving line options are helpful inclusions.

The dearth of suitable hymns for weddings has led me to compose a verse which can be added to the others of "Morning Has Broken," a universally familiar hymn.

> Sing with thanksgiving, God has so formed us
> From the beginning, Two become one.
> Christ in our midst now, Drawing us closer,
> Wedding through this vow, New life begun.

The practice of lighting the unity candle (from two side candles which remain lit, as a sign of continuing individuality of each partner) has been accompanied by another original set of lyrics which may be spoken to instrumental accompaniment to the tune of "Tallis' Canon" or sung as the two lights become one.

> The two together tapers light
> Bring forth a marriage that is bright
> With love and joy which each does share
> Within a home that shows God's care.
>
> All praise to Thee our Lord this hour
> For all the blessings of your power,
> That two who trust you one become,
> The parts made greater in the sum.

When parents of the bride and groom light the side candles before the service, the symbolism is deepened. Commitment is learned and conveyed from one generation to the next. That husband and wife-to-be truly marry into one another's family is beautifully attested to by a "Blessing of the Families,"in place of the "Giving of the Bride." Such wording as "We give our blessing to this union, and receive you into our family and affection," spoken by the parents of the son or daughter to the future spouse expresses mutual acceptance.

The extended family comes into play as the church relationship becomes nurturing, with newly married encouraged to become part of a support group within the congregation. In that fellowship the meaning of *agape* love can continue to be identified and applied.

Other Unions

In more recent years it has become increasingly clear that loving relationships are not limited to marriage. Becoming one is now recognized within a growing number of churches as the issue also pertaining to faithfulness between gays and lesbians. We are all called to appreciate how despite negative references to same same sex relations within the Bible (especially as these threatened the procreation needed to insure Israeli's ethnic survival), Jesus never addressed the subject. Rather his teaching centered upon self-giving love. From that emphasis we can infer that for Christians the issue is not how people use their genitals, but whether they abuse others as persons. Sexual sin consists of promiscuity in contrast to faithfulness.

So while there is no biblical or legal basis for recognizing same-sex partnerships as marriage, there is every reason to celebrate caring relationships which endure, which enable persons to become more fully themselves, and so to know themselves loved and accepted by God. Thus clergy are in a unique position to help strengthen what are for all practical purposes family ties.

The same principle applies to heterosexual couples who have been living together. The day of passing judgment upon them should have long since passed. Yet I find that an increasing number of couples come with the request to have their union blessed in marriage. Somehow making the commitment, in the presence of witnesses, for keeps—all that transforms the relationship. As long as either his or her "fingers are crossed," there is a limit to the depth of intimacy.

The Context of Love

The key question which brings the relationship into focus is what role love plays in marriage. Is it just one factor among many, or is it different?

It helps to visualize marriage as a circle containing a number of smaller circles. Some would place love as one of these, alongside interests, values, sex, children, in-laws, work, money, and religion. But love is more realistically portrayed as the total matrix, in which each of the parts dwells, through which they creatively interact.

This image of the circle or cell should certainly be understood as dynamic. A time dimension would allow for the size of the components to vary, adjustments which love turns into growing opportunities. That which is labeled "religion" means religious practice. But love is the spiritual context. So I do not conclude the counseling without discussing of the issues raised in the following sermon.

The Preaching

Becoming One

Genesis 2:15-25, Mark 10:2-9

Now, it may seem strange to say, but I am enthusiastic about these scriptures. That is not the kind of thing people usually get worked up about—a new car maybe, or a trip to Hawaii in January. But why do these few verses from the Bible produce such an affect?

First of all, the Genesis passage is a beautifully told classic. It speaks so lyrically of God having made the man, and finding that it was not good that he should be alone. "Therefore man leaves his father and his mother and cleaves to his wife and they become one flesh." *They become one.* Now that is word-music!

But more than style is involved. There is depth of meaning which has continued to resupply every generation with insight as to what it means to be a human being and how we do, in fact, become one.

There has been, of course, a controversy over how literally to take this story. But the geography of the Garden of Eden matters less than its spiritual truth. Its truth is not of the same order as whether we descend from the Java Ape Man, but whether we perceive ourselves as persons in communion with one another.

Aspects

Let us, then, focus on the heart of the matter, the innermost mystery of human relationships—how to become one. Usually this union is associated with sexual relationships, an aspect not to be minimized. Interestingly enough, it is not the church which downplays the sexual element. Rather it is in the X-rated world in which the process is under-played. Sex is often reduced to a simple release of physical tension, or, in *Playboy* fashion, to a cool, detached manipulation.

There is nothing particularly new about that. After all, the world's oldest profession has to do with the selling of sex. But what is really new in our time is using sex to sell. You can see it on the ads on TV. Just watch and "feel the fantasy."

The problem with this attempt to isolate sex from love is that it simply does not work. As a psychosomatic being, your body and soul are tied up in one bundle. You cannot give only a part of yourself without frustration. Or, if you use your body in order to breach the loneliness, but without a forthcoming of the whole self, you are lonelier than ever.

The most realistic of all views is that of the Bible which understands "flesh" as more than a bodily function; rather, it is understood as an expression of the whole self. It is biblical inspiration which has led to the insight that sex is what happens more between the ears than between the thighs, that the real four letter word for intercourse is "t-a-l-k."

The humor in Genesis highlights this truth, as the Lord, through "trial and error" helps Adam not to be lonesome. Because it was not good that the man should be alone, he tried offering the company of the fish of the sea and the birds of the air; but none of this was fitting. Finally, by taking "flesh of his flesh," and "bone of his bone," he was given not just a person of the opposite sex, but one who shared his humanity, with whom communion was possible. That is what shatters the isolation. To become one is to share life at all levels, as surely as "God made little apples"—whether in Eden or not.

Take children as what becoming one flesh means. A traditional view is that marriage is the institution intended by God for procreation, it is even more valid to view the birth of children as a fruit of a loving relationship which is its primary purpose. It has been truly said that the best gift that a father could make to his children is to love their mother (and vice versa). Couples always need a life of their own, with children thereby finding fulfillment in relation to boundaries.

There was a couple who was desperately trying to have children who once came asking me to pray for God to grant them their desire. I had to respond that I could not pray for that outcome beyond our control. But I did promise to pray that they might relax and have a joyful sex life. As it happened the wife became pregnant within a month! In such a mysterious way are prayers answered!

Take in–laws as what becoming one flesh means. At the time of marriage, two people are really marrying each other's families far more than they realize. On the High Plains of Texas, there was a newspaper editor who led a crusade, tongue-in-cheek, to establish "Mothers-in-Law Day," just so people could better appreciate the potential in that relationship. After all, it was a daughter-in-law, Ruth, who spoke those immortal words to her mother-in-law, "Where you go, I will go; your people shall be my people; and your God, my God."

So, let us recognize, once and for all, that to become one is more than just a physical matter. That is the biblical insight which stands over against the worldly view of human nature, so well expressed in the lyrics of a Gilbert and Sullivan operetta:

Darwinian man, though well behaved,
At best is only a monkey shaved.

The Unbecoming

If becoming one is not just a matter of "doing what comes naturally," but is a relationship which requires the very best of us, then we would do well to learn from our mistakes. In that light Jesus' teaching on divorce, on the unbecoming, are highly relevant in providing a comparative viewpoint.

As it happened, the divorce controversy raged as fiercely in Jesus' time as does in our own. The assumption then was that a man could always leave his wife. The wives had no rights because they were first the property of their fathers, and then later of their husbands. But the real bone of contention was the grounds for divorce.

There was the strict school, on the one hand, and the *laissez faire* school on the other. The "strict constructionist" claimed that the only way a man could put his wife away was by catching her in the act of adultery. Those with the looser interpretation claimed that if a wife was caught talking to a strange man, or even burned the bread, she could be put away.

Jesus cut through all that quibbling, and went right to the heart of the matter. When he asked, "What did Moses command?", the rabbi replied, "Moses allowed a man to write a certificate of divorce and to put her away." But Jesus rejoined that it was not allowed, but *commanded* that a certificate be written; for this enabled a woman to remarry. Otherwise, she was left without any rights. Jesus, therefore, offered protection to the vulnerable partner, while at the same time recognizing that divorce may be the lesser of two evils. All the while he emphasized that the intention of the Creator from the beginning was that the two should become one in a lasting relationship. The implication of the Lord's teaching is the necessity of working at the relationship.

The effort required was well illustrated in the case of a husband who went to a counselor about his second marriage. Before the first marriage had ended in divorce, he had gone to the same person for help, and now was back again. The counselor asked, "Do you think if you had worked as hard on your first marriage as you have on this one that it would have lasted?" The man replied, "I have to level with you. The first marriage was a 'piece of cake' compared to this one. But now I'm working on myself, rather than trying to change my mate."

Grace

We cannot conclude our thoughts without recognizing that despite all of the hard work, the earning of this relationship, there is a grace around, through and beneath us, which makes possible the effort. The grace comes as a letting go of others in the family, trusting them to the one who brought us together in the first place. It is the reason that a quote of Kahil Gilbran from *The Prophet* is so often used in wedding ceremonies, and so fitting in any worship service.

> But let there be spaces in your togetherness, And let the winds of the heavens dance between you... Even as the strings of a lute are alone, though they quiver with the same music.

Finally, the grace of becoming one is inseparable from the catalyst of sharing a purpose beyond the immediate family. This is unity to be found in God's providing us with a mission—people not so much gazing rapturously into one another's eyes as turning their gaze toward a common goal. They thereby give Christian dimension to the old Chinese proverb:

> If there is a righteousness in the heart, there will be beauty in the character. If there is beauty in the character, there will be harmony in the home. If there is harmony in the home, there will be order in the nation. If there is order in the nation, there will be peace in the world.

Thus, becoming one in all relationships, at all levels, at once fulfills the biblical vision and our deepest need, through the at-one-ment of our Lord. Such union is indeed cause for life-long rejoicing!

Worship

The Practice

Worship and worth go together. It's not just that the origin of one word is to be found in the other, but that worship represents what is of ultimate worth to the people and leaders of a congregation.

Worship is the *sine qua non*—without which there is nothing to a faith community. Worship, while not the only purpose, is, nonetheless, the church's *raison d'être* because no other institution provides such service.

All of the above may seem to belabor the obvious. But it is tempting to take this primary function for granted. For clergy the tendency may be to lapse into liturgical routine, which leaves both leader and the led listless. So the challenge is for ordained people to become spiritually renewed and renewing.

Renewal

It's commonly recognized that a liturgical renewal has been occurring in Christendom, especially since Vatican II stimulated an ecumenical response. In the intervening decades a host of worship books, hymnals and other devotional resources have come off the presses of many denominations. Illustrative of the movement is the standard text in the field, *Introduction to Christian Worship* , whose author, Methodist James F. White, teaches at Notre Dame.

The movement has been twofold in regard to the recovery of traditions long neglected and to the offering of new material which is intended to speak to contemporary worshipers. The latter was especially apparent in the 1960s and 1970s, while the former has emerged more in the 1980s and 1990s.

The pastor, as the liturgical leader, is called to provide guidelines and resources from the faith tradition, while helping mesh these with the needs and expectations of the local congregation. Being "liturgically correct" is less the call of God than to discern meaningful forms and substance of worship.

A worship committee is an instrument to provide a forum to elicit responses from members of the church. Besides monthly meetings to review and preview services, a quarterly feedback gathering is an inviting means to receive input for planning upcoming seasons and services.

But renewal means more than devising such organizationally supportive ways of strengthening the worshiping community. That process is inseparable from the pastor and members finding and practicing their own spiritual direction.

Spiritual Direction

It is through the Catholic tradition, particularly through Ignatius Loyola, that spiritual direction was given clear definition. His *Spiritual Exercises* has long since been adapted and simplified by non-Catholics, and its value has proved immense to a growing number in an age when the term "spirituality" has become common currency.

While that word is subject to trivialization in the excesses of the The New Age, there can be no question that it is at the heart of any vital public worship experience. When the pastor understands his or her role as a guide who fosters the spiritual direction which happens among the people of the congregation, then the "fruits of the Spirit" will abound.

It's been my privilege to have spent sabbatical time at the Program for Christian Spirituality at San Francisco Theological Seminary. While there I had occasion to consult with Sr. Elizabeth

Liebert, whose writings in the field of spirituality have been especially instructive.

Based upon that experience I have had confirmed what I called earlier in my ministry "A Method in Your Gladness." No less valid than the scientific method is a spiritual methodology which involves noticing, naming, nurturing and networking the movement of the Spirit.

The coincidences which bespeak Providence, the feedback from the self and the Other, the inspiration, images and impulses which present themselves—all these surface through contemplation, meditation, journaling, reflection, and conversational prayer. This inner dialogue is of a piece with the worship drama.

The Drama

It was Soren Kierkegaard who caught both the dialogical and dramatic character of public worship. He used the analogy of God, people and liturgist as being like the audience, actor, and prompter respectively (contrary to the usual notion of God being like the prompter, the congregation like the audience, and the liturgist like the actor). In such manner did the Danish philosopher recognize how worship involves performing.

Of course, if worship becomes a performance, as distinct from including a performing element, then the

Worship~Pastor as Prompter

integrity of the worshiping process is compromised. Yet every leader of worship must be clear and comfortable with performing her or his role well, in helping prompt worshipful dialogue with God.

Clergy themselves should serve as role models in this regard. Moreover, the movement from one place to another in the chancel, the uplifting of arms in sacramental action, the laying on of hands in ordination, confirmations, and wedding services, the use of the eyes at all times should bespeak an understanding of how vital is body language in fostering dialogue.

The Dialogue

Because all worship, public and private, is at heart a dialogue, then the pastor's responsibility is to help get that conversation going and flowing. The starting point in worship is adoration, continuing in confession/assurance of pardon, in hearing and responding faithfully to the Word in music and art forms, in scripture, preaching, sacrament and offering. The benediction, fittingly, concludes with the words which send people into the world with a clear sense of mission.

Between the gathering in worship and scattering in service,the pastor will have performed well if persons in the congregation have indeed perceived and felt God's presence, have heard a Word beyond the human voice, and have know themselves called to be instruments of God's service.

The Preaching

From Transcending to Sending

Isaiah 6:1-8

It begins in transcending and ends in sending. That's the account we have of Isaiah in the Temple, as his initial vision of the transcendent God lifts him above and beyond himself. But that exultation does not conclude until he has heard and heeded the call to be sent to his people in life-changing mission.

So is your worship and mine, and ours together, meant to be conformed to that image of the prophet's encounter with the Holy One. Likewise will ours always include elements of confession and forgiveness which issue from glimpsing the glory of God and which result in faithful service.

There is a kind of inner flow in Isaiah's experience which fits the rhythm of grace within and between us. It all begins within a transcending sense of awe.

Transcending

From the time we were children, we have had a primordial sense of God's awesomeness. From awakening to the unimaginably vast cosmos, with its 16-20 billion light year immensity, to the wonder of a "flower by a crannied wall," how can we not be struck dumb?

In the face of what theologian Rudolph Otto called "the numinous," nothing but an approach in silence seems fitting. Before the opening of the Seventh Seal, according to the book of Revelation, "There was silence in heaven for about a half hour." Certainly time in quiet devotion before entering into private or public prayer opens us to that same Spirit, which is also described in the Liturgy of Saint James:

> Let all mortal flesh keep silence
> And with fear and trembling stand...

This "centering," as it's been called, frees us from the all-too-prevalent noise pollution of the world. And like Isaiah, we will no sooner know ourselves to be in touch with Holiness than we become aware of our sin.

Confession

That awareness of our unholiness in the face of total truth is as instinctive as averting our eyes when they happen to turn toward the sun. The Source of all Light exposes our unclean lips and lives. Confession, therefore, is not only "good for the soul," it is essential for the soul not to wither and die.

Of course, T.S. Eliot was right in declaring that humankind cannot bear too much reality. If nothing else, the revelation of God to us in worship stirs us to admit to how much denial we are in.

Yet the transcendent God, whose "robe filled the temple," increasingly fills us with an ever-greater capacity to see ourselves for what we are in God's sight and thereby to make ever more complete confession of sin.

Certainly one of the most creative depictions of sin is the painting of artist Ivan Albright, who entitled one work, "That Which I Did Not Do I Should Have Done." The picture is of a door with a faded wreath upon it, with only a hand shown reaching out, suggesting an after-the-fact situation, perhaps after a death, when it is too late to make amends.

To be a person of "unclean lips" among "a people of unclean lips" is to recognize that for every one sin of commission there are likely to be ten of omission. Standing silently by when others are being degraded with racial slurs is to be as culpable as those hurling the insults.

Moreover, we may think of sin as something strictly personal, like smoking or drinking. But our participation in corporate sin does far more damage, whether it's in making our polluted input into the air, or by our apathy, by which we give tacit consent to the conditions making for homelessness and hopelessness.

No wonder Isaiah declares, "Woe is me!" But no sooner has he confessed his uncleanliness than he awakens to how he has seen the Lord of hosts and yet is still allowed to live. Then the catharsis begins.

Cleansing

Just how cathartic confession can be is given graphic expression by the seraph who is described as flying to the altar, taking a live coal with tongs and touching the prophet's tongue. That's the painful, yet cleansing action of forgiveness. "Now this has touched your lips, your guilt has departed, and your sin is blotted out."

The assurance of pardon in public worship each Sunday may seem insipid compared to such a soul-searing experience as that of Isaiah. Yet no one of us need let that declaration of forgiveness be spoken without making personal identification with the merciful image given to us. For us as Christians, no more humbling yet hopeful words could be sounded than these:

> In this is the good news, that while we
> were yet sinners, Christ died for us.

Imagine that! While we were *yet sinners* (not after we proved ourselves deserving), Christ died for us. Repeat that! Believe that! Act on that in mission!

Sending

While the truth hurts, it is also liberating. It frees us to be on the go as surely as Isaiah heard and heeded the call, "Whom shall I send?...Here am I! Send me!"

Psychologist Robert Coles in his book *The Call to Service: A Witness to Idealism* cites Dorothy Day as an example of "awesome altruism." He took a group of Harvard University freshmen to meet her, two years before her death, at The Catholic Worker Soup Kitchen. She told her visitors, "If I pray by making and serving soup, I feel I'm praying by doing. If I pray by saying words, I can sometimes feel frustrated."

When one of the freshmen questioned how she could tell whether it was really God who had sent her on this errand of mercy, she spoke of how answers came in prayers. "He has sent us the thoughts, the ideas. They all don't just belong to us. He lives in our thoughts, the Lord does."

Then she referred the Harvard student to *The Imitation of Christ,* saying that Thomas a' Kempis, as an obscure priest, wrote of his struggle to be a good person, centuries ago. When the student responded, "I'll try to find the book in Cambridge and read it," she playfully added, "I hope you can find it there."

May we all be able to find ourselves imitating such followers of Christ, as he continues to call in worship and service. In the name of the transcendent Lord, make your confession, receive his cleansing Word, and be prepared to go forth saying, "Here am I! Send me!"

APPENDIX
Aerial View of the Bible

Histories	*BOOKS* *Prophets*	*Poetry*	*Dates*	*Events*
			1800	Abraham called into Palestine
				(Period of Patriarchs)
			1300	Moses leads Exodus from Egypt
				(Period of the Judges)
			1000	David unites tribes into Kingdom
				Kingdom splits 922
Genesis				
Exodus			900	
Numbers				Elijah opposes Ahab and Jezebel
Leviticus			800	
Deuteronomy	Amos			
Joshua	Hosea			
	I Isaiah (1-39)			Israel falls to Assyria 721
Judges	Micah		700	
I & II Samuel				King Josiah seeks to reform Judah
I & II Kings	Jeremiah/Lamentations		600	
	Ezekial			Judah falls to Babylonia 586
	II Isaiah (40-55)			(Babylonian exile)
	Haggi			The Persian, Cyrus, conquers Babylon
	Zechariah 1-8			frees Jews, new Exodus begins
	III Isaiah (56-65)		500	
I & II Chronicles				Ezra and Nehemiah rebuild Jerusalem
Ezra			400	
Nehemiah		Job		
Ruth	Jonah	Song of Songs		
	Joel			Palestine conquered by Greeks 331
	Malachai	Psalm	300	
	Zechariah 9-14	Proverbs		
		Ecclesiastes	200	
	Daniel			Maccabean revolt 165
				Essenes at Qumran — Dead Sea Scrolls
			100	
				Palestine conquered by Romans 63
				Jesus born 4-8 B.C.
	Epistles	*Gospels*	0	
			30	Death and resurrection of Christ
				Conversion of Paul
			40	
I & II Thess.			50	Paul's first missionary journey
				Paul's second journey
I Cor. & II Cor. 10-13				Paul's third journey
Galatians, II Cor. 1-9				
Romans				Paul taken as captive in Rome
Ephesians, Colossians			60	
Philemon and Philippians				Paul's death
		Mark	70	Jews revolt; Jerusalem destroyed
		Matthew	80	
		Luke-Acts		
		John	90	
Hebrews and letters of John				First systematic persecution of Christians
James				under Domitian 96
Revelation				
I Peter				
I & II Timothy, Titus and Jude			100	
II Peter			150